Computer Wings

Mail Manager

Course Book

Syllabus Version 1.0

First Edition 2009

ISBN 9780 7517 5757 6

British Library Cataloguing-in-Publication Data
A catalogue record for this book is available from the British Library

A joint publication from:

Q-Validus Ltd.

NovaUCD   t: + 353 1 716 3742
Belfield Innovation Park   e: info@computerwings.com
University College Dublin   w: www.computerwings.com
Dublin 4   w: www.q-validus.com
Ireland

BPP Learning Media Ltd.

BPP House, Aldine Place   t: 0845 0751 100 (within the UK)
London W12 8AA   t: + 44 (0) 20 8740 2211
United Kingdom   e: learningmedia@bpp.com
                                    w: www.bpp.com/learningmedia

Computer Wings® is a registered trademark of Q-Validus Limited in Ireland and other countries. This Computer Wings approved training material may be used in assisting Candidates to prepare for their Computer Wings certification test.

Candidates wishing to sit Computer Wings certification tests are required to pre-register for the programme. Candidates may register at any Authorised Centre.

Without registration, certification tests cannot be taken and a Computer Wings certificate or any other form of recognition cannot be awarded.

For any further information about Computer Wings visit www.computerwings.com

CONTENTS

What is Computer Wings?

Computer Wings is an exciting new practical computer skills certification programme for real world tasks and roles in the modern workplace.

The certification delivers knowledge and skills in a range of areas. The Computer Wings programme assists candidates to achieve increased efficiency, higher standards of output, and greater levels of collaboration, and improved user confidence.

The Computer Wings programme covers the key functions within an organisation such as planning, project management, communication, marketing, IT, online business and process flows.

The Computer Wings programme is a flexible, scheme that allows Candidates to choose the module or modules which are most appropriate to their current or future roles.

Computer Wings provides a total programme solution including registration, automated testing and certification and as supporting training materials.

For further information visit www.computerwings.com

Scottish Qualifications Authority (SQA) endorsement

The Computer Wings qualification scheme is mapped to the UK National Occupational Standards (NOS) and is endorsed by the Scottish Qualifications Authority (SQA). The Computer Wings programme has been credit rated and levelled for the Scottish Credit Qualifications Framework (SCQF).

Mail Manager has been officially designated as SCQF level 7 with 6 credit points. To see the SCQF level and credits for all other Computer Wings Modules visit http://www.computerwings.com/endorsements

Get certified

You now have your Computer Wings Course Book, which is designed to bring your skills to the next level. The next step is to prove your competencies by taking the Computer Wings certification test. Computer Wings is endorsed by the Scottish Qualifications Authority (SQA) www.sqa.co.uk, a world renowned awarding body.

Register for your test

To gain your Computer Wings certification you need to register for your test with a Computer Wings Authorised Centre.

Computer Wings certification tests are only available through Authorised Centres. For further information visit www.computerwings.com

Computer Wings overview

Computer Wings® is an exciting new computer skills training and certification programme. The programme consists of ten stand alone modules which focus on the productivity skills required in today's rapidly changing economy.

The Computer Wings certification programme comprises the following modules:

Project Manager

Plan, resource, execute and manage mid-sized projects to deliver high quality, well defined, organised results on time and on budget.

Mail Manager

Communicate and collaborate more effectively by becoming proficient in the use of email software to manage organisational scheduling and communication.

Diagram Maker

Enhance effective business communication by using diagram tools and image editing applications to create diagrams, images and conceptual schemes.

Newsletter Publisher

Produce professional quality newsletters, brochures, eshots or leaflets to support marketing activity and organisational communications.

Presenter Pro

Enhance business communications by developing the skills to create and deliver attractive, persuasive, and audience focused presentations.

Web Creator

Create and maintain informative and user-friendly websites to support internal and external communications.

Web Optimiser

Develop Search Engine Optimisation (SEO) skills to support and improve traffic, create more impact, and generate higher sales.

Web Analyser

Use web analysis tools to measure the appeal of a website, view the origin of visits and referrals, and generate reports about website activity.

IT TroubleShooter

Develop the IT administration skills required to deal with hardware, software, memory and network issues in small IT network environments.

IT GateKeeper

Recognise important software, hardware and network security considerations in order to protect small IT network environments.

Computer Wings benefits

The Computer Wings certification programme enables Candidates to develop their skills and confidently address computing applications relevant to their needs.

The Computer Wings certification programme delivers:

- A recognised and valuable qualification.
- Practical skills, competencies, and knowledge.
- Awareness of good practice, efficient and productive use of applications.
- Confidence to produce effective and professional looking outputs.
- Improved returns on human and ICT investments.
- Validation of skills and knowledge as evidenced by certification.
- A match between Candidate skills and organisational needs.
- Enhanced collaborative skills within an organisation.
- Improved productivity through more efficient use of office applications.
- Improved communication across the organisation.

Content validation

Q-Validus works with Subject Matter Experts (SME's) and renowned international awarding bodies and international partners, to develop and provide Computer Wings, which reflects a comprehensive and recognised skills and knowledge standard.

Computer Wings Course Books are developed by SME's across the range of specialist domains.

Ongoing content validity of Computer Wings Syllabus standards definition is maintained by the Syllabus Expert Group (SEG) using the Q-Validus online Content Validation Database (CVD), a bespoke software tool for standards validation. Expert feedback and comment from around the world, in respect of Computer Wings Syllabus measuring points, is collated and recorded in the Content Validation Database. The current Computer Wings Syllabus Version is Syllabus Version 1.0. The ongoing standards validation process for Computer Wings supports the continuing applicability and relevance of Computer Wings.

Experts wishing to provide technical comments and feedback in relation to Computer Wings Course Books, or seeking to participate as experts in relation to the Computer Wings Syllabus standards definition, should contact: technical@computerwings.com

Computer Wings Mail Manager overview

Computer Wings is an internationally recognised computer and ICT skills standard. Computer Wings training and certification programmes help Candidates work more effectively by developing computer and ICT skills that deliver valuable productivity benefits.

Computer Wings Mail Manager is a certification in the area of personal information systems management. The core product referenced in this Course Book version is Microsoft Outlook 2007. The Mail Manager course anticipates Microsoft Exchange as the mail server software.

The Computer Wings Mail Manager certification validates Candidate skill and knowledge in using email software to facilitate effective communication and collaboration across the organisation, as well as with clients, and other stakeholders.

Mail Manager is designed to provide practical competence with the major features and functions of Microsoft Outlook and enable Candidates to manage their email, schedule, tasks, and their time.

Candidates shall:

✓ Use email software to work, communicate and collaborate effectively.

✓ Set application user preferences to optimise workflow.

✓ Define categories to help organise communications and projects.

✓ Set email security measures for junk mail, attachment handling.

✓ Manage the view environment for email, tasks, calendars, fields, panes.

✓ Create and assign tasks, set reminders and priorities.

✓ Make appointments, update schedules and share calendars.

✓ Update contact details, create address lists.

✓ Organise communication folders and flag urgent email items.

✓ Set Out of Office response messages.

✓ Reply on behalf of a colleague.

✓ Apply organisation email policies.

✓ Set email backup / archive intervals.

✓ Be aware of security issues and related user responsibilities with email.

Mail Manager Syllabus

Category	Skill area	Ref.	Measuring point
2.1 START	*2.1.1 Preferences*	2.1.1.1	Set send and receive options.
		2.1.1.2	Setup mail accounts.
		2.1.1.3	Set contact options.
		2.1.1.4	Select message format (HTML, plain text).
		2.1.1.5	Set signature, spelling and stationery options.
		2.1.1.6	Set mail start-up options.
		2.1.1.7	Set mail with default text editor.
		2.1.1.8	Create a new profile, use a different profile.
		2.1.1.9	Set properties for mail, personal or contacts folders.
	2.1.2 Views	2.1.2.1	Select different fields for views.
		2.1.2.2	Group, sort items in a view.
		2.1.2.3	Modify views, column size, order.
		2.1.2.4	Create a new view, modify an existing view.
		2.1.2.5	Delete a view.
	2.1.3 Categories	2.1.3.1	Organise, set a category list scheme.
		2.1.3.2	Assign a category.
		2.1.3.3	Change a categorisation.
		2.1.3.4	Apply a categorisation when creating an email.
2.2 SEND/ RECEIVE	*2.2.1 Create*	2.2.1.1	Create a new message.
		2.2.1.2	Save a message draft.
		2.2.1.3	Attach a file with different security options.
		2.2.1.4	Recognise a digital signature in a message.
		2.2.1.5	Compress a file attachment before sending.
		2.2.1.6	Set different voting and tracking options.
	2.2.2 Deliver	2.2.2.1	Set different delivery options and take account of message size transmission limitations.
		2.2.2.2	Recognise common error messages about mail delivery from the local server, or the ISP (Internet Service Provider).
		2.2.2.3	Send a message using different stationery.
		2.2.2.4	Send a message using an email template.
		2.2.2.5	Send a message on behalf of another user.
		2.2.2.6	Use a web-based form of making comments or contact, or a web-based email application.
	2.2.3 Inbox	2.2.3.1	Use, customise the Reading Pane.
		2.2.3.2	Use header, two line, AutoPreview feature.
		2.2.3.3	Set attachment handling security settings.

Category	Skill area	Ref.	Measuring point
		2.2.3.4	Open and save attachments.
		2.2.3.5	Decompress a file attachment.
		2.2.3.6	Flag, categorise a message.
		2.2.3.7	Reply to, forward a message.
2.3 ORGANISE	2.3.1 Notes	2.3.1.1	Set different notes views.
		2.3.1.2	Create notes.
		2.3.1.3	Change note appearance.
		2.3.1.4	Categorise a note.
		2.3.1.5	Save a note.
		2.3.1.6	Send a note.
		2.3.1.7	Print a note.
	2.3.2 Tasks	2.3.2.1	Set different task views: timeline, table, day/week/month, arrangement views.
		2.3.2.2	Set different task options.
		2.3.2.3	Create a new task.
		2.3.2.4	Create a recurring task.
		2.3.2.5	Assign a task to a person, or a group.
		2.3.2.6	Accept, decline a task. Reassign a task.
		2.3.2.7	Check task status.
	2.3.3 Setup	2.3.3.1	Set the Out of Office Assistant.
		2.3.3.2	Show alerts.
		2.3.3.3	Set junk mail (SPAM) filter rules.
		2.3.3.4	Create, configure public folders within the inbox.
		2.3.3.5	Set automatic redirection of incoming emails to specified folders, or other mail accounts.
		2.3.3.6	Use the Search function.
		2.3.3.7	Apply different search criteria.
2.4 SHARE	2.4.1 Calendar	2.4.1.1	Create appointments in the calendar.
		2.4.1.2	Add appointment reminders.
		2.4.1.3	Add different notes for free / busy information.
		2.4.1.4	Create, modify a recurring, one-off appointment.
		2.4.1.5	Delete appointments, events.
		2.4.1.6	Email a calendar.
		2.4.1.7	Interact to book, confirm, or re-schedule a meeting.
		2.4.1.8	Print calendar in table, memo or calendar format.

Category	Skill area	Ref.	Measuring point
	2.4.2 Team-up	2.4.2.1	Share, view calendars.
		2.4.2.2	Send calendar information to a contact.
		2.4.2.3	Create a meeting from scratch.
		2.4.2.4	Create a meeting from an appointment.
		2.4.2.5	Invite different people, request resources for the meeting.
		2.4.2.6	Check meeting attendee response status.
		2.4.2.7	Send a meeting update.
		2.4.2.8	Be aware of different communication options such as instant messaging, VoIP.
2.5 CONTACTS	*2.5.1 Create*	2.5.1.1	Create a contact.
		2.5.1.2	Switch between different contact.
		2.5.1.3	File, save a contact.
		2.5.1.4	Add phone, mail, web and email information.
		2.5.1.5	Enhance contact details with a picture.
	2.5.2 Organise	2.5.2.1	Create a contact from an email message.
		2.5.2.2	Find a contact categorise a contact: business, personal etc.
		2.5.2.3	Share a contacts folder.
		2.5.2.4	Print contacts using different print styles.
		2.5.2.5	Create an address list.
		2.5.2.6	Use contacts to create an address list, a distribution list and make changes.
		2.5.2.7	Include a contacts folder in an address book.
		2.5.2.8	Import data from an existing email client.
		2.5.2.9	Import data from other applications.
2.6 SECURITY	*2.6.1 Backup*	2.6.1.1	View folder, item sizes.
		2.6.1.2	Backup mail items, folders.
		2.6.1.3	Set backup, archive intervals.
		2.6.1.4	Use available automatic archive tools.
		2.6.1.5	Exclude some items from backup.
		2.6.1.6	Restore archived data.

Category	Skill area	Ref.	Measuring point
	2.6.2 Secure	2.6.2.1	Recognise significant security considerations for the organisation with regard to email clients.
		2.6.2.2	Recognise common email issues such as SPAM, junk mail, chain mail and viruses, and adjust security settings to help deal with these.
		2.6.2.3	Set security settings on a personal folder.
		2.6.2.4	Request, set up a certificate.
		2.6.2.5	Send a message using a certificate.
		2.6.2.6	Send, receive a signed message. Send an encrypted email message.
		2.6.2.7	Save a senders' public key.
		2.6.2.8	Set different email security or privacy options.
		2.6.2.9	Set attachment handling and macro security properties.
		2.6.2.10	Set virus protection.
	2.6.3 Laws & guidelines	2.6.3.1	Be aware of data protection legislation or conventions in your country.
		2.6.3.2	Be aware of copyright laws and their impact for downloading content from the Internet.
		2.6.3.3	Be aware of 'netiquette' conventions and protocols for confidentiality when communicating with others.
		2.6.3.4	Recognise guidelines and procedures set by the organisation.
		2.6.3.5	Recognise the significance of disability / equality legislation in helping to provide all users with access to information.

Mail setup for administrators

This section covers the Send/Receive group options which can only be carried out by those who have network privileges.

Some tasks, in particular send and receive intervals with your Internet Service Provider (ISP) are probably carried out by your network administrator, who setup the accounts, the user groups and the intervals at which email will be dispatched and received.

It is useful for any Outlook user to understand how their email accounts are set up or preconfigured by their network administrator.

When using Send/Receive groups, you can specify various options:

- Email accounts included when sending or receiving email messages.

- Intervals at which sending or receiving emails occurs.

- Size limit for emails received.

- Off-line send and receive schedule.

When you have set your Send/Receive group options, you will only need to change them if you have a new account or if your working arrangements change, for example home working.

To create a Send/Receive group:

1. Select *Tools* and select *Send/Receive*.

2. Click *Send/Receive Settings* and select *Define Send/Receive Groups*.

3. Within *Send/Receive Groups*, select *New*.

4. Type a name for the Send/Receive group and click *OK*.

5. The new group is displayed.

6. Click *Close*.

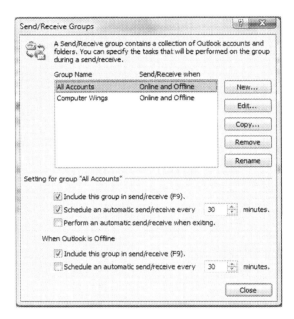

When you have organised your email accounts, you can schedule your email communications as required.

Settings for Send / Receive groups

You can specify various communication settings for each Send/Receive group such as scheduling different connection times or intervals to suit the account or accounts included in a group.

To specify communication settings for a Send/Receive group go to the *Send/Receive Groups* dialogue box as outlined previously:

1. Select the Send/Receive *Group Name* from the list.

2. In the *Send/Receive Groups* box, select the *Include this group in send/receive (F9)* check box.

3. Depending on your group communication requirements, specify the appropriate setting:

- Schedule an automatic send/receive of your emails and the frequency for this event to occur, for example, every 30 minutes.

- Send/Receive emails before exiting Outlook.

- Specify whether you want emails to be sent while working offline and the frequency of these emails.

4. Click *Close*.

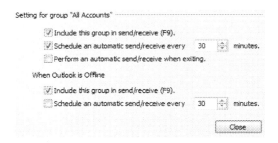

Setting up an email account

To set up a new email account on Outlook:

1. Select *Tools* and select *Account Settings*.

2. In the *Accounts Setting* dialogue box, click *E-mail* and select *New*.

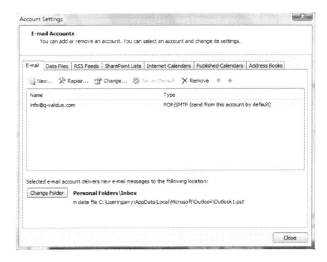

3. In the *Add New E-mail Account* dialogue box, select the *Microsoft Exchange, POP3, IMAP or HTTP* email service option and click *Next*.

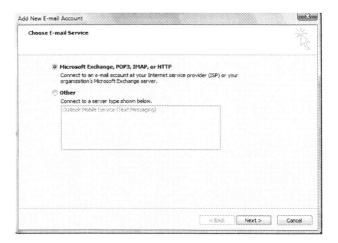

Email service protocols specify how email is retrieved.

- Post Office Protocol (POP3) which delivers email from the server without leaving a copy of the email.

- Internet Message Access Protocol (IMAP4) retains a copy of the email on the server.

4. In the *Add New E-mail Account* dialogue box, type your name, email address and password twice to allow automatic connection to the host email server.

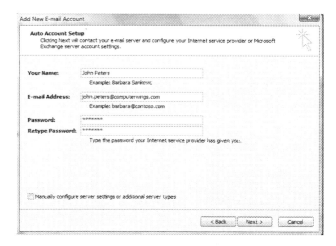

5. For an Exchange Server 2007, click *Next* to search for your server settings and to retrieve your email account settings. A confirmation message is displayed when your account is set up.

For a non-Exchange Server 2007 set up, select *Manually configure server settings or additional server types*. You will need to contact your network administrator for the mail set up details.

6. Click *Next*, follow the remaining steps to complete the procedure.

Start

1

| Start |
| Send and receive |
| Organise |
| Share |
| Contracts |
| Security |

Measuring points

- Set send and receive options
- Setup mail accounts, and address books
- Set contact options
- Select messages format (HTML, plain text)
- Set signature, spelling and stationery options
- Set mail startup options
- Set mail with default text editor
- Create a new profile, use a different profile
- Set properties for mail, personal or contacts folders

- Select different fields for views
- Group, sort items in a view
- Modify views, column size, order
- Create a new view modify an existing view
- Delete a view
- Organise, set a category list scheme
- Assign a category
- Change a categorisation
- Apply a categorisation when creating an email

Introduction

Microsoft Office Outlook is a key part of your personal information management system. Outlook will help you to work more effectively by enabling you to manage your communications, work schedule, activities and contacts in a collaborative work environment.

This chapter covers setting up email formats, applying professional signatures and stationery. How to organise your views with Outlook as well as setting up email profiles is also covered.

Email formats

Different message formats provide for different message views, while a plain text message will have the highest chance of being viewed by all recipients, it does not offer any of the other formatting effects.

You can specify how email messages are viewed. The following formatting options are available:

- *HTML*: supports formatting such as bullets, alignment, and colours. This is the default in Outlook and maintains any formatting when sending and receiving a message.

- *Rich Text Format (RTF)*: supports the formatting between different Microsoft applications.

- *Plain Text*: delivers and receives text without any formatting. Pictures are also not supported but can be included as attachments.

To set formatting options for your emails:

1.   Select *Tools* and select *Options*.

2.   Click *Mail Format* tab.

3.   Select the required *Message format* option.

4.   Click *OK*.

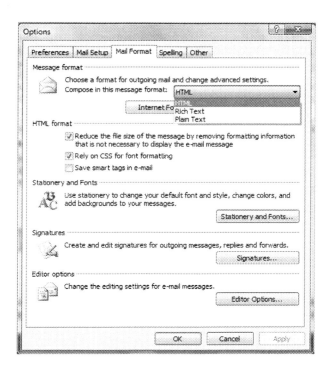

 If you know that certain recipients can only receive emails as plain text, you can include this setting in the contact details for this recipient.

Attachments included in HTML formatted emails or plain text formatted emails are detailed under the Subject line as shown:

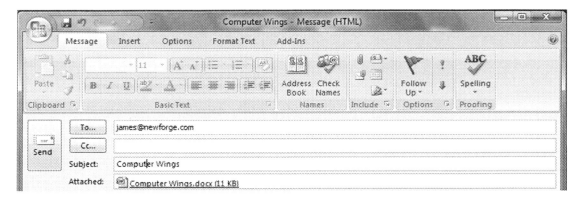

Attachments included in RTF formatted emails are displayed in the body of the message.

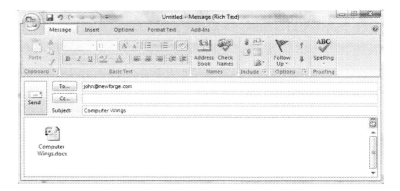

 There are many ways in which commands can be carried out with different software products: Menus, toolbar icons, a keyboard command, or a right-click can all be used. A visual approach is taken as the main task pathway for learning here; for example, making text bold could be achieved by using a toolbar icon or the keyboard shortcut: *Ctrl+B*. Candidates and Trainers should be aware that in this Course Book a menu or dialogue based approach is used as the preferred learning pathway.

Signatures, spelling and stationery

You can easily customise the appearance of your emails in Outlook by applying a corporate signature or a stationery theme to ensure a professional and consistent appearance. It is also important to spell check emails before they are sent.

Signature

An email signature can enhance and promote your organisation's corporate identity by providing useful contact and company details.

To create a signature:

1. Select *Tools* and select *Options*.

2. In the *Options* dialogue box, select *Mail Format* and click *Signatures*.

3. In the *Signatures* and *Stationery* box, click *E-mail Signature*.

4. Click *New* to create a new signature.

5. Type a name to identify the signature and click *OK*.

 Different signatures can be used for different email accounts, for example your personal signature can be your default signature when you want to respond to an 'info email' from an info email account you can create and associate a different signature. In the *Signatures and Stationery* dialogue box choose the *E-mail Account* menu, to associate a signature with the relevant account.

6. Complete the signature details in the area provided. You can specify formatting options for individual lines in your signature by applying different colours and fonts.

7. Click *OK*.

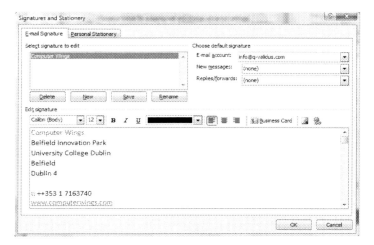

You can review and modify your signature as required by repeating the steps described above.

Spelling

It is a good practice to spell check all your emails prior to sending them to ensure that the correct spelling and grammatical convention is used, to reinforce the professional image of the organisation and to ensure the email is easy to understand.

To set the spelling and grammar check as always on, use the following steps:

1. Select *Tools* and select *Options*.

2. In the *Options* dialogue box, click *Spelling*.

3. Enable the *Always check spelling before sending* check box. If you do not want to spell check existing information when replying to a message, you should also enable the *Ignore original message text in reply or forward* check box.

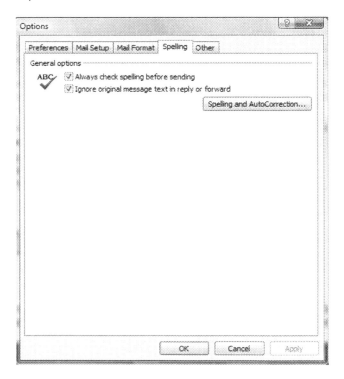

 If you are working on a different computer and the spelling and grammar check is not turned on, you can activate this feature by pressing F7.

 It is often useful to create a custom dictionary to ensure that certain words such as your name, product names, brands or technical terms that are often used in your organisation, will not be highlighted when doing a spell check.

Stationery

You can choose a background theme to apply a professional look to all your emails. Using stationery options to enhance the email content with additional colours, imagery or branding. A suite of default stationery is provided in Outlook.

To apply a stationery theme:

1. Select *Tools* and select *Options*.

2. In the *Options* dialogue box, click *Mail Format*.

3. Select *HTML* from the *Compose in this message format* list, in order to enable the stationery format.

4. Select *Stationery and Fonts*.

5. Click *Personal Stationery* and select *Theme*.

6. Select the required theme or stationery option. The illustration shows a '*Soft Blue*' (stationery) theme.

7. Click *OK*.

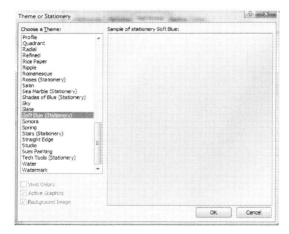

Once a theme has been applied, all email messages will open and display with the background theme selected.

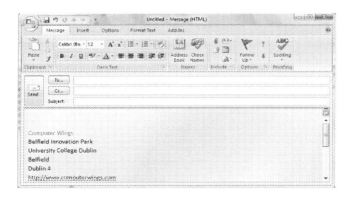

Setting startup options

You can choose how you want Outlook to work when you open the application, by selecting the email folder you want displayed, how your emails will be displayed and the kinds of reminders you will get as you work, including warnings and alerts.

To set Outlook start up preferences:

1. Select *Tools* and click *Options*.

2. Click the *Other* tab and select *Advanced Options*.

3. Select the required general settings, for example if you want the *Inbox* displayed when you open Outlook or if you want the *Calendar* displayed.

4. Click *OK*.

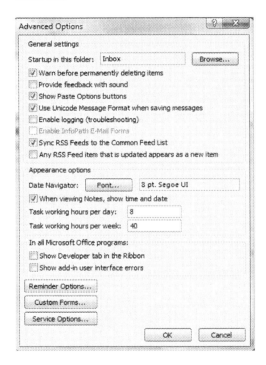

 By default, Outlook 2007 uses the Microsoft Word 2007 email editor and it cannot be changed to another application. However, you can select the email format, HTML, RTF or Plain Text as previously described.

Using email profiles

Email profiles are used to create individual identities associated with a specific email and where they are stored. You can use multiple profiles with Outlook 2007. This is useful if you want to separate your personal emails from business emails, or where there are multiple individuals using a single computer.

An email profile is created when you initially open Outlook. It is often useful to create an additional email profile for a new product, brand, service, event or an everyday info email account.

To create an additional email profile:

1. In Windows, click *Start* and select *Control Panel*.

2. Select the *Mail* icon.

Mail

3. Within *Mail Setup* click *Show Profiles*.

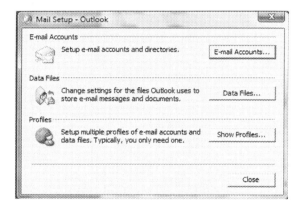

4. The *General* tab displays details of any profiles existing on your computer.

5. Click *Add* to create a new email account profile.

6. Type a name for the new profile.

7. Within *Add New E-mail Account*, type the email address to associate with the profile and the required display name (the name which will be visible to a recipient), the precise email address and the password provided by your ISP.

8. Retype the password to verify it is correct.

9. Click *Next* and complete the remaining steps to complete the procedure.

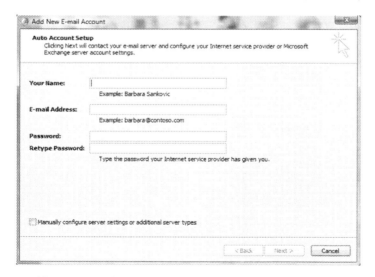

 You may need to contact your network administrator to obtain the ISP details.

Switching profiles

When you launch Outlook and you have more than one profile, a drop-down menu will provide you with your profile choices.

You can also set a default profile which will automatically open on Outlook launch.

To set a default profile:

1.   Click *Start* and select *Control Panel*.

2.   Select the *Mail* icon.

3.   Within *Mail Setup* click *Show Profiles*.

4.   In *Mail*, select the profile you wish to use within the *General* tab.

5.   Select the *Always use this profile* option to switch to the required profile from the list menu as your default. If you want to be prompted to select a profile when Outlook is opened, select the *Prompt for a profile to be used* option.

6.   Click *OK*.

7.   Click *Close*.

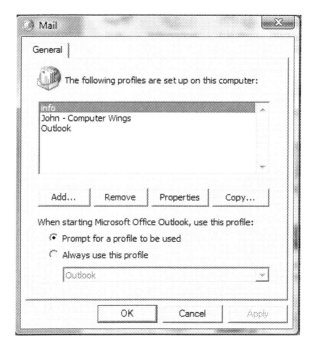

 You will need to close and restart Outlook when you want to switch between profiles.

Setting folder properties

You can specify how you want to work with the different Outlook folders and customise how items are displayed. This can help you to work more efficiently, for example, you can set the Inbox folder settings including folder size to ensure that you do not encounter problems when your Inbox exceeds the size guidelines as specified by your network administrator.

To set Outlook folder properties:

1. Select and right-click the *Inbox* folder or alternatively, select *File* and click *Properties*.

2. Click the *General* tab of the folder's *Properties* box and select *Advanced* to display the settings for your personal folder (.pst).

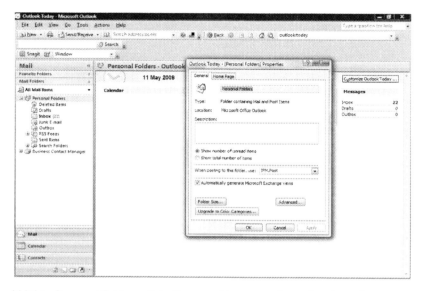

3. Within *Personal Folders*, click *Compact Now* to reduce the size of your personal folder file.

Viewing options

You can organise how you want Outlook to display information to ensure easier and rapid viewing of emails. You can display the list of folders in a *Navigation Pane* or use the *Reading Pane* to preview an email.

Navigation Pane

The Navigation Pane is a sidebar panel that displays all your Outlook folders in a hierarchical view. You can display the contents of individual folders and move quickly between files and folders as necessary.

To activate the Navigation Pane:

1.   Select *View*.

2.   Click *Navigation Pane*.

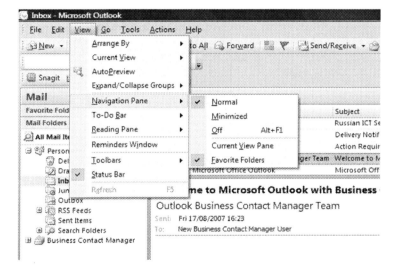

Reading Pane

You can preview email messages without opening them by using the Reading Pane.

To activate the Reading Pane:

1. Click *View*.

2. Select *Reading Pane*.

3. Select *Bottom* to display the *Reading Pane* below your messages, the email currently selected is displayed.

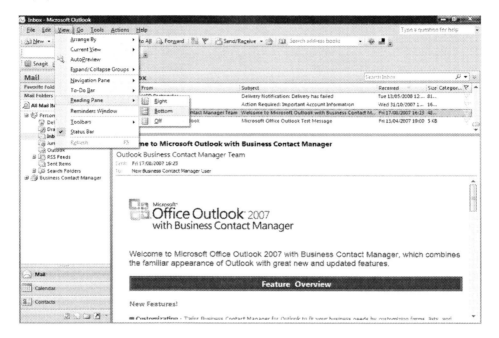

 Attachments contained with a message are not activated when you preview the message in the *Reading Pane*, for that reason you can use the *Reading Pane* to check that a message is not SPAM or junk mail, which could contain potentially dangerous threats such as viruses or .exe files.

Warning: Treat any unsolicited emails with caution to avoid compromising your own computer and other computers in your organisation.

AutoPreview

You can check email content using the AutoPreview feature in Outlook. AutoPreview displays the first three lines of unread messages in the Inbox.

To activate AutoPreview:

1.   Select *View*.

2.   Click *AutoPreview*.

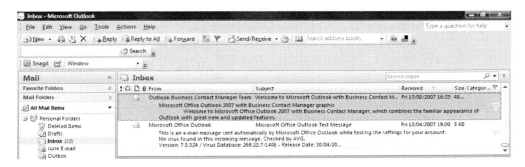

Additional views

There are a whole range of additional views available, under View and *Current View*, such as messages from the last seven days, messages which are unread, and messages including documents etc.

Sort and group

You can sort and group emails in your Inbox to help manage your messages. Sorting is a very effective way of managing your email, and can be very useful for quick email retrieval. Grouping can be a very useful feature and can add significant productivity benefits.

Sort

A sort can be performed from any of the columns currently used in the view displayed, for example when you click on the sender's name; the emails are grouped according to the sender details.

When you click on a column view such as date *Received,* the emails are shown from the most recently received to the oldest, clicking on the label again refreshes and reverses the sort order for emails with the oldest emails first.

Group

You can specify that you want to display emails based on a group. For example, if you sorted your emails based on recipients or date of receipt.

1.   Select *View* and select *Arrange By*.

2. Click *Show in Groups*. The emails are grouped based on their size ranges.

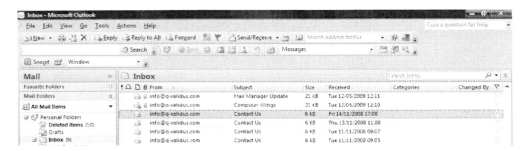

 Grouping emails is also useful where you have created folders for managing your emails. When you group a set of emails from a particular contact, you can select and move the entire set to a unique folder created for correspondence with that particular contact.

Modifying views

You can modify the standard view for information displayed in Outlook to create a customised view that best suits your viewing and work requirements.

To create a view:

1. Select *View* and click *Current View*.

2. Click *Define Views*.

3. Click *New* to create a custom view.

4. In *Create a New View* type a name for the view and specify how you want the view organised, for example, based on a table of information.

   You also need to specify to whom the view is available, if this view is only for you, select *This folder, visible only to me* option and click *OK*.

5.	In the *Customize View: New view* dialogue box, click *Fields*.

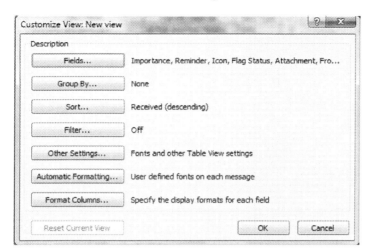

6.	In the *Show Fields* dialogue box, some pre-defined fields are shown. Add to these from *Available fields* as required. You can also remove fields and change the order.

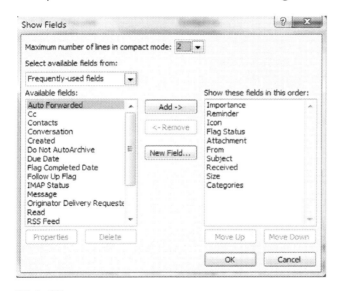

7.	Click *OK*.

In addition you can manage and further customise views you have created with *Custom View Organizer*.

To modify a view:

1.	Select *View*, click *Current* and click *Define View*. The *Custom View Organizer* dialogue box is displayed.

2.	Select the view and click *Modify* to customise it, for example to sort the information into ascending or descending order.

3. Click *Apply View*.

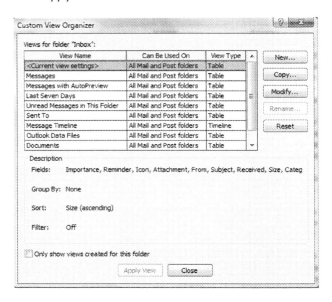

Changing column widths

You can make a quick adjustment to the amount of information displayed by varying the column widths. To vary the width of a column, click and drag the separator line that divides the column headings.

You can also adjust column widths by right-clicking on a column header and selecting *Format Columns*.

The *Format Columns* dialogue box displays the various fields in the current view and you can specify individual widths for the fields.

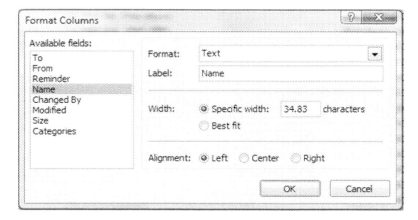

You can also change the column titles and vary the alignment of the information in columns.

Changing column order

You can change the column order in an Outlook view by clicking on the column header and dragging it to a new location. This is useful if you want, for example, to check a series of emails from a specific sender based on the email subject line.

Using categories

Categories allow you to quickly organise information into meaningful groups, for example, you can categorise emails and meeting arrangements for an individual person or client organisation.

Outlook provides a set of colour categories as a default and you can add additional categories as required.

Before you begin using *Categories* in Outlook, you need to identify the categories you wish to use.

The first step involves defining appropriate categories, such as:

- Work

- Hobby

- Family

- Friends

Next you need to include a *Category* column to the current view:

1. Click on a column heading and select *Customize Current View* from the menu displayed.

2. Select *Fields*.

3. Select *Categories* from the list of *Available Fields* displayed, and click *Add*.

Now that there is a *Category* field within the current view you can add, display and edit the available categories:

1. Click *Edit* and select *Categorize*.

2. Click *All Categories*.

3. The available colour categories are displayed. You can rename the existing categories, for example, changing the name *Blue Category* to *Organisation*.

4. Click *New* to create a new category. You can specify a name and colour for the category.

5. Click *OK* to add it to the category list.

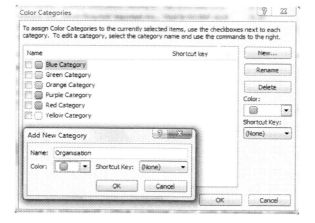

You are prompted to change the default details when you initially apply a default category to an Outlook item.

You can assign existing items to categories by right-clicking on the item and selecting *Categorize*. You can now select one or more *Categories* for the selected item.

You can automatically assign a category to an incoming email, by following the steps outline:

1. Select and right-click on the email.

2. Select *Message Options*.

3. Click *Categories*.

4. Select a *Category*.

5. Click *Close*.

To change the category assigned to an email or apply additional categories:

1. Select and right-click on the email.

2. Select *Categorize* to display the categories list.

3. Click the required new category.

4. Click *OK*.

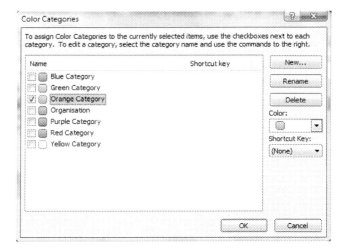

Quick Quiz

Select the correct answer from the following multiple-choice questions:

1   You wish to change how your emails will display, which feature tool will allow you to do this:

   a   *Field chooser*

   b   *Viewer*

   c   *Format*

   d   *Setup*

2   What does the acronym POP stand for?

   a   Point of Presence

   b   Post Office Protocol

   c   Personal Office Protocol

   d   Permanent Office Protocol

3   Which email message format supports the use of bullets, alignments and links in an email?

   a   Rich Text Format

   b   Plain Text Format

   c   Mail Tab Format

   d   Message Tab Format

4   You would like to view a message without opening it. Which one of the following menu commands should you choose to activate this option?

   a   *View > Reading Pane*

   b   *View > Toolbars*

   c   *View > Print*

   d   *View > Arrange By*

5   Complete the statement by inserting the missing word.

A _____ is a specific group identifier that you can define and assign to any number of Microsoft Outlook items.

a   Preference

b   Reminder

c   Flag

d   Category

Answers to Quick Quiz

1   a   *Field chooser*

2   b   Post Office Protocol

3   a   Rich Text Format

4   a   *View > Reading Pane*

5   d   Category

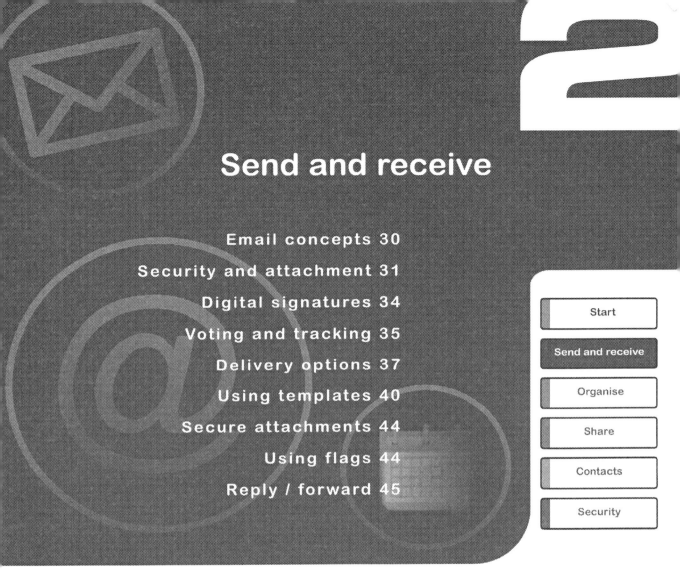

Send and receive

Start

Send and receive

Organise

Share

Contacts

Security

Measuring points

- Create a new message
- Save a message draft
- Attach a file with different security options
- Recognise a digital signature in a message
- Compress a file attachment before sending
- Set different voting and tracking options
- Set different delivery options, and take account of message size transmission limitations
- Recognise common error messages about mail delivery from the local server or the ISP (Internet Service Provider)
- Send a message using different stationery

- Send a message using an email template
- Send a message on behalf of another user
- Use a web-based form for making comments or contact, or a web-based mail application
- Use, customise the Reading Pane
- Use header, two line, auto-preview feature
- Set attachment handling security settings
- Open and save attachments
- Decompress a file attachment
- Flag, categorise a message
- Reply to, forward a message

Introduction

Outlook offers a range of useful features to help you communicate professionally and securely.

This chapter covers working securely with email attachments, and using digital signatures. Voting and tracking for scheduling with groups, as well as flags, alerts and delivery options are also covered.

Email concepts

Email message exchanges are based on the Simple Mail Transfer Protocol (SMPT) which is the Internet standard for message transmission over the Internet Protocol (IP) networks. Emails can be stored on either the server or the client computer depending on the setup.

Transmission from the client computer to the server is normally based on SMPT while transmission from the server to the client is likely to be based on common protocols such as POP3 or IMAP.

Email content has evolved from consisting of text-based information to media-based attachments containing audio and video clips.

Create

To create and send an email:

1.   Select *New* and click *Mail Message,* or press *Ctrl + N.*

2.   Type your message and specify the recipient from your contact list or by entering the email address.

      If you have a file to attach click on the *Attach File* toolbar icon:

3.   Click *Send.*

Saving a draft

You can save a draft of an email at any stage as you work in Outlook, and return to it later. Draft messages are saved in the *Drafts* folder. Outlook automatically saves draft emails to this folder every three minutes.

To modify the AutoSave settings for Outlook:

1.   Select *Tools* and click *Options.*

2.   Click *E-mail Options* and select *Advanced E-mail Options.*

3.   Modify the required settings as necessary.

4.   Click *OK*.

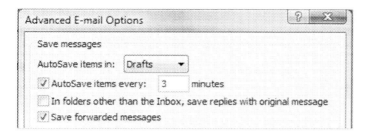

Security and attachments

With the growth of the Internet based communications and the increasing threat of viruses and other malicious software, Microsoft have implemented a whole range of security features in Outlook 2007 to help deal with these threats. The *Trust Center* is the Outlook 2007 security control centre for attachment handling.

It is every user's responsibility, as well as the organisation itself, to work safely with email. The tools for every user to help increase security in attachment handling are maintained within the *Trust Center*.

Viewing attachments is enabled by default in Outlook. For added security you can turn off the attachment preview feature in the *Trust Center*.

To turn off the attachment viewing feature:

1.   Select *Tools* and click *Trust Center*.

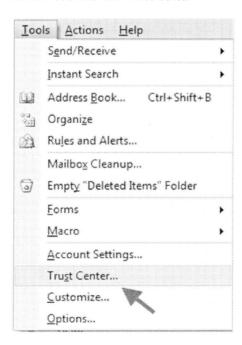

2.   In the *Trust Center* dialogue box, select *Attachment Handling*.

3.   Click the *Turn off Attachment Preview* check box.

4.   Click *OK*.

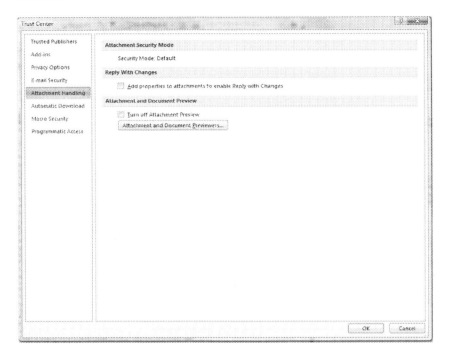

There are common sense practices which help protect your computer. You should ensure that you only open attachments received from trusted sources. If you receive an email that you suspect contains a virus notify your network administrator immediately.

Version control and security

The *Trust Centre* offers an important feature when you are collaborating with colleagues on Word documents and you wish to track and merge all changes. For track changes to work you need to retain the properties information for your document. Properties information can include name, address, email, organisation etc.

However, for security reasons you may not wish to transmit this information with your attachment, although this will mean track and merge features will not be available.

To turn off properties in a Word document:

1.   Select *Tools* and click *Trust Center*.

2.   In the *Trust Center* box, select the *Attachment Handling* option.

3.   Deselect the *Add properties to attachments to enable Reply with Changes* check box.

Compressing attachments

You can compress email attachments using the *New Compressed (zipped) Folder* feature. You can use this feature when sending an email containing large file attachments. You can either attach previously compressed files to an email, or compress them before transmitting the file in an email.

To compress files and send them in an email:

1. Navigate to the folder containing the file, or a folder containing a set of files, that you want to include in an email.

2. Right-click to display the actions available and select *Send To*.

3. Select *Compressed (zipped) Folder*.

    A zipped version of the file is created with the same filename but with the file extension *.zip*.

4. Now if you wish to attach the .zip file by email, either select:

    a. The zipped folder you have created and right-click it.

    b. Select *Mail recipient* from the list of actions. A new email is opened with the zipped file contained in the list of attachments.

    or

    a. Create a new email in Outlook.

    b. Click *Attach File*.

    c. Navigate to the folder containing the compressed file.

    d. Select the file to include it as an attachment in your email.

    e. Complete and send the email.

It is good practice to use compression features when sending large file attachments in emails and also to know your own file size limits for sending and more importantly for receiving. The reliance on email for everyday communication is increasing, for example, a marketing team who wish to transmit graphic and various media files including audio and video clips, would need to consider these file size restrictions. Large files may not be delivered which is why it is important to know that the size of an email includes both the size of the message and any attachments.

You can improve email transmission time and reliability by ensuring that you do not exceed the file storage space imposed by your ISP or by your network administrator in your organisation.

Digital signatures

Digital signatures enable you to authenticate the sender of an email message. This is particularly useful where you need to verify the identity of the person or organisation sending an email. A digital certificate can be obtained through a recognised certification authority such as VeriSign Inc.

When you 'digitally' sign an email, you are applying your own mark including your unique certificate and public key information. With this information, the email recipient will know that the message has not been sent by an unreliable source and that it has not been changed during transmission.

Checking a digital signature

You can authenticate the sender of a message by reviewing their digital signature.

To verify a signature:

1. Select and open the required digitally signed email.

2. Check the sender details in the *Signed By* status line.

    The signature is:

    - Valid if the signature icon is displayed:

    - Invalid if the signature icon is underlined and displayed as an exclamation mark.

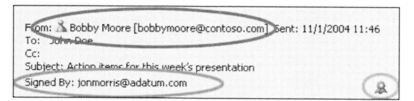

Voting and tracking

The voting feature is very useful when for example, you are coordinating an event or meeting and you want a group to make a decision on a suitable date or venue. You can include voting buttons in your email to facilitate this. You can also do questionnaires, surveys and polls using this feature.

 Voting and polling requires a Microsoft Exchange Server 2000, Exchange Server 2003 or Exchange Server 2007 account. If you are using an email account assigned by your organisation, you can check the type of account you have been assigned by contacting your network administrator.

To create and send an email containing voting buttons:

1. Select *New* and click *Mail Message*.

2. Type your message.

3. Click *Options* and select *Use Voting Buttons*.

4. Select the type of voting to apply:

    *   *Approve; Reject*

    *   *Yes; No*

    *   *Yes; No; Maybe*

    *   *Custom* enables you to specify voting button names based on the content of your message, for example polls or surveys

5. Complete your message content, select the recipient(s) and select *Send*.

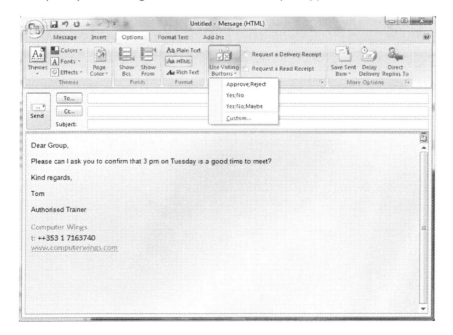

To respond to an email that uses voting buttons:

1.   Select your response from the choices available.

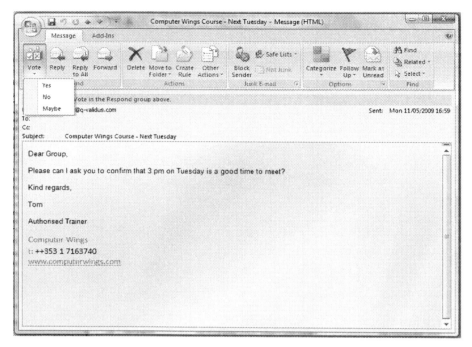

2.   You can either select:

    a.   Select *Send the response now* option to send the response without any comment.

    b.   Select *Edit the response before sending option* to add a comment to your response.

3.   Click *OK*.

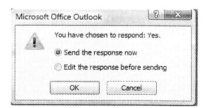

Your response is transmitted to the sender and its details are recorded in the message information bar.

The responses to an email poll are automatically compiled and you can review them using the original polling message.

To display the current list of responses:

1.   In your *Sent items* folder, select and open the original message.

2.   Click the *Tracking* tab to review the responses.

You can reopen the original email at any stage to obtain updated details. The information bar also contains updated totals of responses.

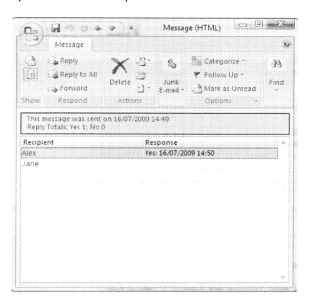

Delivery options

You can specify different delivery options when sending emails to highlight an email to one or more recipients. This means that if you want to alert a recipient that an email needs their immediate attention, you can flag it as being of high importance. To flag the level of importance of an email before you send it, click the *Message* tab and select the level of importance:

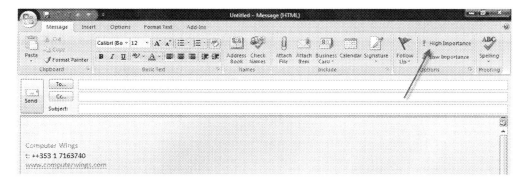

The message and an icon to indicate its level of importance is highlighted in the email.

It is advisable to restrict your use of this flag to messages that require urgent or immediate attention. It is considered poor email etiquette to send all emails with a high importance flag.

Sensitivity level

Outlook provides a useful feature that enables you to set the sensitivity level of an email to alert one or more recipients about how an email's content should be treated. For example, you may want to alert a recipient that the information contained in an email is of a sensitive nature. This is a useful feature when you are covering a colleague's email.

To change the sensitivity level of an email:

1.   Right-click on the message, click *Message Options*.

2.   In the *Message Options* box, open the *Sensitivity* list and select either:

   * *Normal*

   * *Personal*

   * *Private*

   * *Confidential*

The email is flagged with the selected sensitivity level.

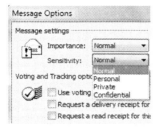

Copy etiquette

In certain cases, you may want to copy one or more recipients on an email, this is known as sending a Carbon copy (Cc). This is useful where the information you are communicating requires the direct response of the email recipient, but you also need to inform other colleagues in your organisation about the email content. In many cases, a copy recipient does not need to action the content but is being notified about it. Each email recipient can also view a list of the other individuals who have been copied on the email.

You can use Blind carbon copy (Bcc) to send an email without displaying the list of recipients. Each email recipient can not view the list of the other individuals who have been copied on the email.

Sometime the *Bcc* address bar is not displayed by default. You can display the entry line for *Bcc* under the *To* and *Cc* contact entry lines by selecting *Show Bcc* from the *Options* tab when creating a message.

It is important to consider how you use different copy features. Bcc is often useful for external communications where you do not wish to show the full email copy list for confidentiality and privacy reasons. For internal communication Bcc is considered poor email etiquette, in certain circumstances.

Scheduling delivery

You can schedule when you want your emails to be sent. This is useful when you want to send an email at a certain time.

To schedule the delivery of an email:

1.   In a new message, select the *Options* tab.

2.   In *Options* click the *Delay Delivery* icon.

3.   Specify the date and time when you want the email to be sent.

If the email is only valid up to a certain period, you can select the *Expires after* check box and specify the date and time after which the email should no longer be sent.

4.   Click *Close* and send as normal.

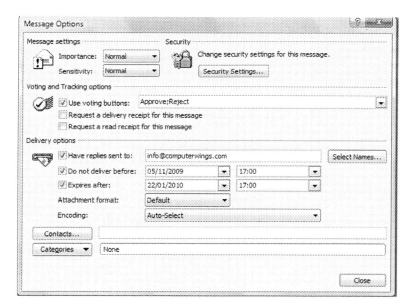

Using templates

Using Outlook templates, you can create standard email messages that need to be sent on a regular basis. You can use a template for a regular meeting or project, and then edit it before sending to change some details, for example, the date and meeting venue details.

To create an email template:

1.   Open a new message as usual.

2.   Type your message and specify the recipient from your contact list or by entering the email address.

3.   In the *Save As* dialogue box, select *Outlook Template* in the *Save As* type list (an .oft file).

4.   Type a name for your template and click *Save*.

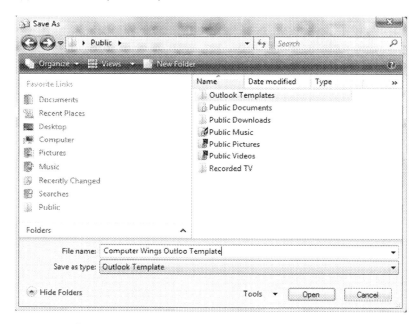

To access a template you created:

1.   Select *Tools*, click *Forms* and click *Choose Form*.

2.   The *Choose Form* dialogue box is displayed in the *Look In Field*. Select *User Templates* in *File System* and click *Browse* to navigate to a folder containing a specific message template file.

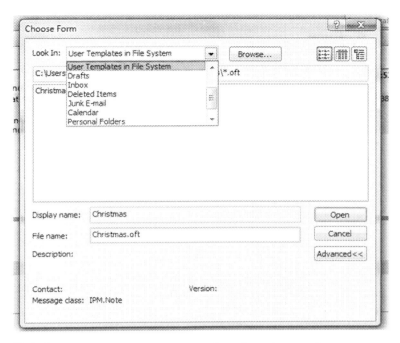

3. Click *Open* to create a new message based on the template.

4. Edit the email template as required before sending. These changes only apply to the email being edited. If you want to make changes to the template, you must open the template from *Forms* and apply and save changes to the template file.

5. Click *Send*.

Reading Pane

You can use the Reading Pane to display emails in your Inbox without opening the email. You can quickly select different items in your Inbox which are then displayed in the Reading Pane.

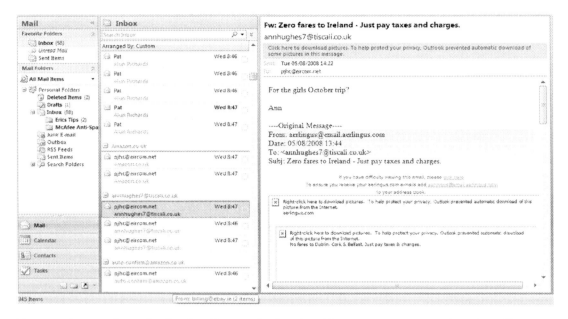

You can change where the Reading Pane is displayed and how you want to work with it. To work with the Reading Pane:

1. Select *View* and click *Reading Pane*.

2. Select the location for the *Reading Pane* by selecting either *Right* or *Bottom*.

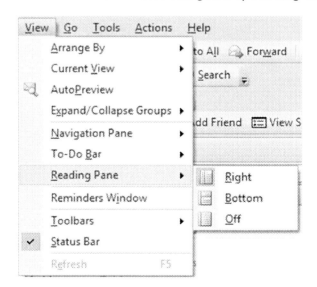

3. Select *Tools,* click *Options.*

4. Select the *Other* tab, click *Reading Pane.*

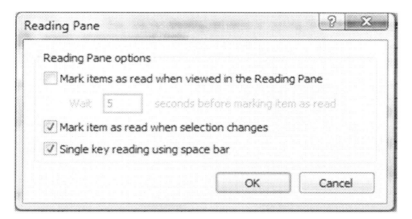

5. Specify the required *Reading Pane* settings.

6. Click *OK.*

You can safely review the content of an email using the Reading Pane as any attachments containing possible viruses cannot be opened or activated.

Secure attachments

You can open email attachments by double-clicking on the attachment name. Before you open any email attachment, you need to consider any virus risks, especially when they are from an unknown source.

To check an email attachment before opening it:

1. Preview the email using the Reading Pane.

2. Select *Save Attachments* and specify the location where you want to store the attachment.

3. Navigate to the folder and check the attachment for any possible security threats using your antivirus applications.

If the attachment is compressed, you can decompress it using the relevant application and then open the individual files.

Using flags

You can use flags in Outlook to set reminders for working with an email. Flags help you to identify and manage emails and their associated activities. Setting flags means that you can manage and prioritise your activities.

To access the available flags, select the flag icon from the toolbar, the available flags are displayed.

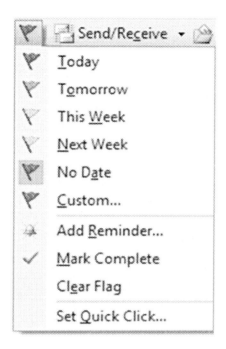

 Flagged messages are displayed in the *For Follow Up* search folder.

Select the required flag. You can change a status of a flagged message by right-clicking on it and then changing the flag status. You can view any Outlook items you have flagged in the *For Follow Up* search folder.

Reply / forward

You respond to emails by selecting either:

- *Reply* to send your response to the sender only.

- *Reply to All* to send your response to both the original sender and to all other people included in the copy list.

- *Forward* to send your response on to someone who was not on the original email distribution.

When you use the *Forward* option, the email including any attachments is sent to the recipients that you specify.

When you respond using *Reply* / *Reply to All* you can add additional recipients in either of the fields as required.

Quick Quiz

Select the correct answer from the following multiple-choice questions.

1   You are working in the Inbox, what opens when *Ctrl + N* are pressed.

   a   A new note

   b   A new contact

   c   A new message

   d   A new appointment

2   As a security precaution, you wish to preview attachments in your incoming mails. Which one of the following menu commands allows you to control this feature?

   a   *Tools > Trust Centre*

   b   *Tools > Customise*

   c   *Tools > Macros*

   d   *Tools > Account Settings*

3   Complete the statement by inserting the missing word.

   When sending an email, the names of recipients are not visible when placed in the ____ address line.

   a   Cc

   b   Bcc

   c   To

   d   From

4   You would like to send a message on a specific date. Which one of the following sequence commands will allow you to control this functionality when you are in a new message?

   a   *Options > Delay Delivery*

   b   *Options > Security options*

   c   *Options > Voting options*

   d   *Options > Attachment options*

Answers to Quick Quiz

1   c   A new message

2   a   *Tools > Trust Center*

3   b   Bcc

4   a   *Options > Delay Delivery*

Organise

Start

Send and receive

Organise

Share

Contact

Security

Measuring points

- Set different note views
- Create notes
- Change note appearance
- Categorise a note
- Save a note
- Send a note
- Print a note
- Set different task views: timeline, table, day/week/month, arrangement views
- Set different task options
- Create a new task
- Create a recurring task

- Assign a task to a person, or a group
- Accept, decline a task. Reassign a task
- Check task status
- Set the out-of-office assistant
- Show alerts
- Set junk mail (SPAM) filter rules
- Create, configure public folders within the inbox
- Set automatic re-direction of incoming email to specified folders, or other email accounts
- Use the Search function
- Apply different search criteria

Introduction

Outlook provides a wide range of features to help you organise and manage your work activities in a logical, coordinated and effective way.

This chapter covers the main collaboration features in Outlook, so that you can effectively manage and track the progress of individual work activities assigned to team members in your organisation.

Using the Out of Office Assistant, viewing alerts, using notes and creating rules and filters for managing, as well as protecting your email environment, is also covered.

Creating a note

With *Notes* you can attach a note reminder to an Outlook item, for example to provide additional information for a task or activity.

To create a note:

1. Select *File,* click *New* and click *Note,* alternatively press, *Ctrl+Shift+N.*

2. Type the information in your note.

3. Click the *Note* icon in the *Notes* box and click *Close.* The note is saved in the *Notes* folder.

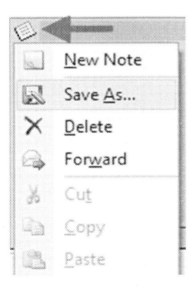

Saving a note

To save a note in a folder that contains related information:

1. Select the *Note* icon.

2. Click *Save As*.

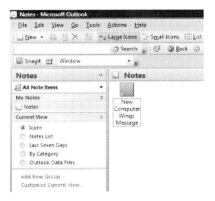

3. Choose a folder location for the note.

4. Type a name for the note and select the appropriate format for saving the note, normally *Outlook Message Format*.

5. Click *Save*.

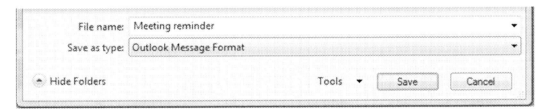

Formatting notes

You can change the format of note as you require.

To change the appearance of notes:

1. Select *Tools* and click *Options*.

2. In the *Preferences* tab, under *Contacts and Notes* select *Note Options*.

3. In the *Note Options* box, specify the colour you want to apply to your note.

4. Choose the size and font style that you want to use for your note text.

5. Click *OK*.

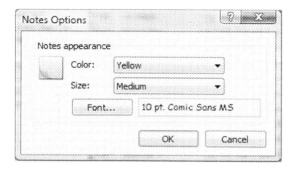

Categorising notes

You can use the *Categorize* feature to assign a colour category to your notes for example, to indicate a particular product or service.

To assign a colour category:

1. Click the *Note* icon.

2. Click *Categorise* and select the colour category for your note.

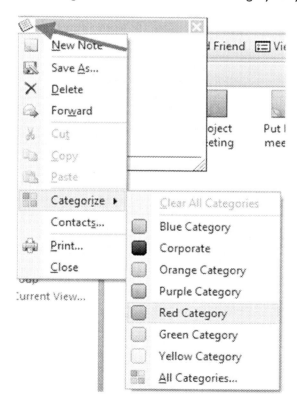

Sending and printing

You can view, email and print notes at any stage while you work in Outlook. To view existing notes, select the *Notes* folder, in the left hand viewing pane. You can choose from the different options how you want your notes to display:

- *Icon view*

- *Notes List*

- *Last Seven Days*

- *By category*

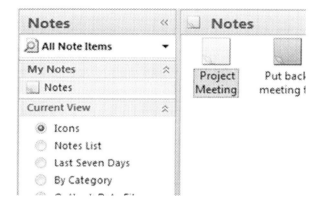

You can also send a note to one or more recipients, to do this:

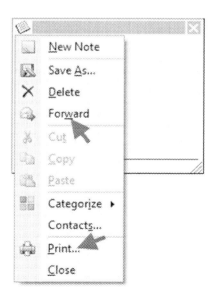

Actions

▶ 1. Click the *Note* icon.

▶ 2. Select *Forward*.

You can also print a note, to do this:

▶ 1. Click the *Note* icon.

▶ 2. Select *Print*.

Creating tasks

Tasks allow you to set and manage individual activities that need to be completed, and also assign priorities and completion dates.

To create a task:

1. Select *File* and click *Task*, or press *Ctrl+N*.

2. Type a name for the task in the *Subject* text box.

3. Set the *Start date* and *Due date* timeline for the task.

4. Click *Save*.

5. Click *Close*.

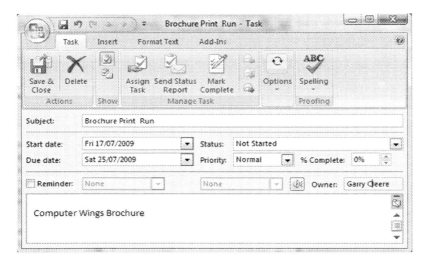

Recurring tasks

If there are certain tasks that you perform regularly, for example, a project status report, you can set a recurring flag.

To create a recurring task:

1. Select *File*, click *New* and select *Task*, or press *Ctrl+Shift+K*.

2. Type a name for the task in the *Subject* text box.

3. Click Recurrence.

4. In the *Task Recurrence* box, select the appropriate options:

   - The frequency pattern for the task, for example, *Daily, Weekly, Monthly* or *Yearly.*

   - The day on which the task is flagged to recur.

   - The new flag should be generated so that it is visible for your attention, *Regenerate the new task ... week(s) after each task is completed.*

   - Set the range of occurrence during which the task occurs based on the start date, the number of occurrences and the actual end date.

5. Click *OK.*

6. Click *Save & Close.*

When you open a recurrent task in the *Task* list, a time stamp is displayed at the top of the box containing the start and end dates for the recurrent task.

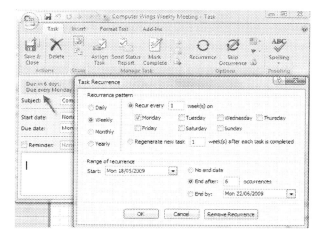

Assigning tasks

When you have created a task, you can assign it to another person in your organisation for completion. This involves emailing the task to the appropriate individual.

Outlook tracks the progress of the task, when it is completed, a completion report is sent. You can easily assign and manage tasks effectively for any project.

To assign a task:

1. Open a new task.

2. Select *Assign Task* in the *Manage Task* options in a new task on the ribbon.

3.   In the *To* field, specify the recipient that you want to assign the task from your contact list.

4.   Type a name for the task in the *Subject* text box.

5.   Specify a start date and completion date for the task.

     You can use the *% Complete* setting to indicate if you have already partially completed the task.

6.   Select the tracking options for the task:

     • *Keep an updated copy of this task on my task list*

     • *Send me a status report when this task is complete*

7.   Click the *Recurrent Task* icon for a recurring task.

8.   Click *Send*.

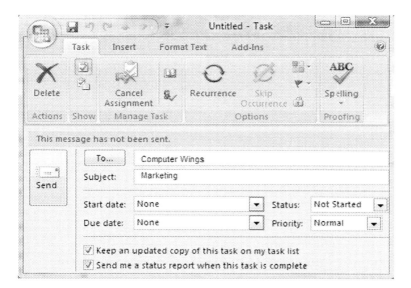

Accept / decline tasks

When you receive a task request, you can review the task details to check whether you are available to accept the task. You can either accept or reject the task.

To respond to a task request:

1. Select and open the task.

2. Click the *Task* tab in the *Manage Task* group.

3. Depending on your response, select the appropriate option:

    *   Click *Accept* to take ownership of the task and complete it as requested.

    *   Click *Decline* to reject the request and inform the person assigning the task that you cannot complete the request.

4. Select the *Edit the response before sending* option and type your comment.

5. Click *Send*.

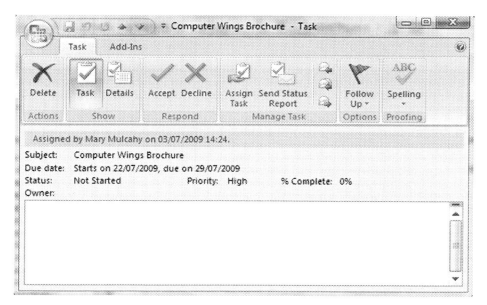

 Assigning a task to an individual, means you transfer ownership of the task to that person. If the recipient declines a task, the ownership is only transferred back to you when you return the task to your task list.

Managing tasks

Reassigning a task

If a task is declined, you can reassign the task to a different individual by repeating the steps previously described under 'Assigning tasks' and selecting a different recipient from your contact list.

Viewing tasks

To view the progress of an assigned task:

1.   Open the *Task* list.

2.   Click *View* and select *Current View*.

3.   Select *Assignment*.

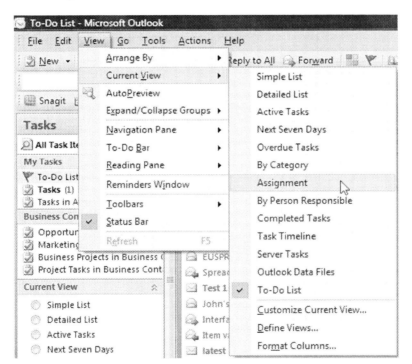

Monitoring tasks

You can use the different task views in Outlook to organise how you want to display task information.

To change how information is displayed:

1. Click *Tasks* or click *View* and select *Current View*.

2. Select the required task view you require from the list, for example, if you want to view detailed information about tasks, select *Simple List*.

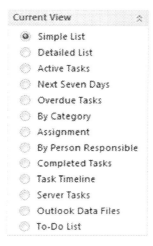

Task timeline

Use the task timeline to display your task over a given interval, week, month etc.

Completed tasks

You can review a list of tasks that have been completed by selecting *Completed Tasks* from the *Current View* list. This view not only shows all completed tasks and when they were due, it also shows if they were early or late.

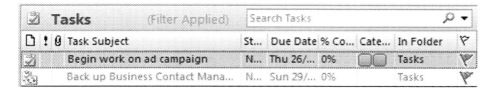

Overdue tasks

You can display a list of overdue tasks and check on their progress by selecting *Overdue Task* from the *Current View* list.

 You can import a series of tasks into Microsoft Project from Outlook using the export feature.

Display options

To work effectively with tasks, you can change how your different tasks, *Overdue* and *Completed* items are displayed.

To change how tasks are displayed:

1. Click *Tools* and click *Options*.

2. Select *Preferences* and select *Task Options*.

3. In the *Task Options* dialogue box, specify your colour preferences for overdue and completed tasks.

4. Select the following tracking options:

    *   *Keep updated copies of assigned tasks on my task list*

    *   *Send status reports when assigned tasks are completed*

5. Click *OK*.

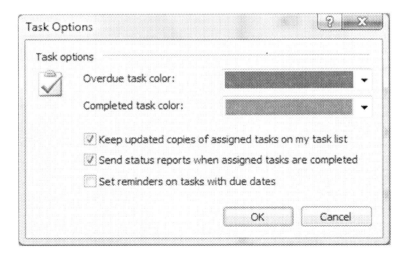

Out of Office Assistant

The Out of Office Assistant feature is a valuable way to communicate to anyone who sends you an email that you are at work but unavailable, on leave or out at an event etc. You can also provide contact details for a colleague who will assist with any queries in your absence and the duration of time that you will be unavailable.

To activate the Out of Office Assistant:

1.   Select *Tools*, click *Out of Office Assistant*.

2.   Select the option *I am currently Out of the Office*.

3.   Select *AutoReply* and specify *Once* to ensure that your message is only sent the first time you receive an email from the sender.

4.   Add the information you want to include in your response.

   •   You can set up a different auto-reply for internal and external emails. You can also choose the required dates at and exact time.

 The Out of Office Assistant feature is only available when Outlook is supported by the Microsoft Exchange Server version.

Desktop alerts

You can set desktop alerts to notify you when you receive emails, meeting or task requests. You may choose not to use this feature all the time, but it is useful if you are expecting an important email or urgent email. By default, the desktop alerts feature is not activated in Outlook.

To activate the alert:

1. Select *Tools* and click *Options*.

2. Click the *Preferences* tab and select *E-mail Options*.

3. Click *Advanced E-mail Options*.

4. Select *Desktop Alert Settings*.

5. Select how long you want the alert to appear on the desktop for and how transparent it should be. With an audio alert you will need to choose the volume and type of alert you wish to use.

6. Click *OK*.

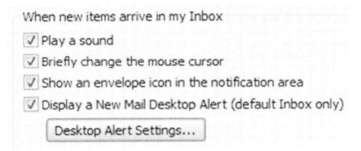

 The desktop alerts feature is only available for email accounts based on the Microsoft Exchange Server and POP3 profiles.

Using email filters

As with any type of communications, paper or electronic, you will receive unsolicited emails that you consider junk mail. With email, this form of unsolicited communications is also known as SPAM.

Outlook incorporates a *junk email* filter so that emails identified as junk mail are moved to a *Junk email* folder.

Setting filters

You can set the level of filtering to apply for incoming emails. By default, the filter is set to *Low*. This incoming email filter setting means Outlook considers it as junk mail. You can change the default setting to a level you consider more appropriate.

To change the email filter settings:

1. Select *Tools* and click *Options*, select *Preferences*.

2. In *Junk E-mail Options*, click the *Options* tab.

    Specify the filtering protection level you want to apply to your emails. If you want the lowest level, select *Low*. With this setting, most junk email will be detected but you may need to check the *Junk* folder to ensure that regular email is not included.

3. Specify any other required protection level settings for how you want the detected junk emails to be handled.

4. Click *Apply* and *OK*.

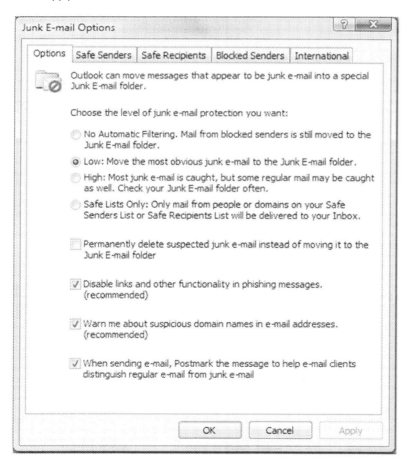

Blocking emails

You can also block emails from one or more senders. These messages are automatically moved to the *Junk E-mail* folder, where you can then make a judgement about whether an email is junk or not.

To block an email address:

1. Select *Tools* and click *Options* select *Preferences*.

2. Select *Junk E-Mail Options* and click the *Blocked Senders* tab.

   The list of any senders or domains previously blocked is displayed.

3. Click *Add* and type a new email address or domain name that you want to add to the list.

4. Click *OK* as required.

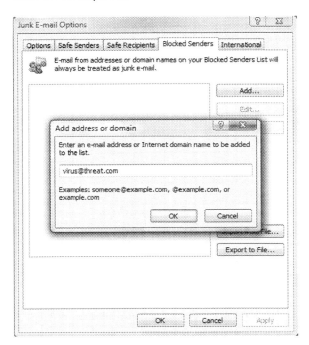

 Also in the *Junk E-mail Options* dialogue box you can go to *Safe Senders* to designate email senders or organisations as safe, this is known as a 'white list'.

Using rules

You can organise and manage your emails using rules. Rules provide for how incoming emails are dealt with, based on some criteria you set, a typical example is moving all meeting requests into one folder.

You can use the *Rules Wizard* to quickly create rules. The *Rules Wizard* automates the steps involved and provides a list of options for defining the rule based on existing templates.

To activate this feature:

1. Select *Tools* and click *Rules and Alerts*.

2. Click *New Rules* to start the *Rules Wizard*.

3. Complete the steps:

    a. Categorise the rule based on whether you want to:

        - *Stay Organised*

        - *Stay Up to Date*

        - *Start from a Blank Rule* to create a completely new rule

    b. Edit the values in the rule description. The values are underlined and you can overtype them to replace with the values you want applied in the rule.

4. Click *Next*.

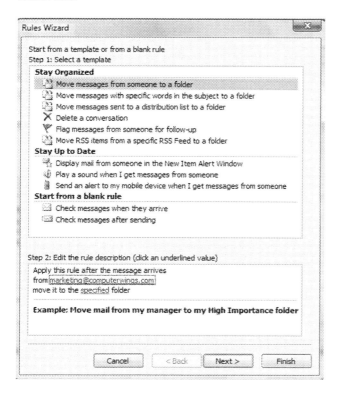

5. Type a name for the rule.

6. Specify when you want the rule applied.

7. Review and edit the rule.

8. Click *Finish*.

Using instant search

You can use the Instant Search feature in Outlook to quickly locate specific emails or information.

To set up Instant Search:

1. Click *Tools* and select *Instant Search* or press *Ctrl+E*.

2. Click *Instant Search*, a search box now appears in the top right hand corner of your inbox.

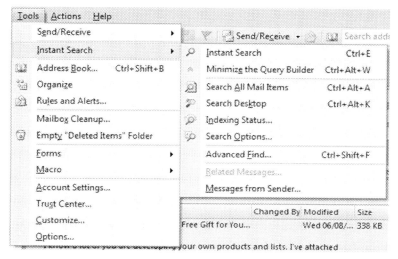

3. Enter your search phrase in the *Search* text box.

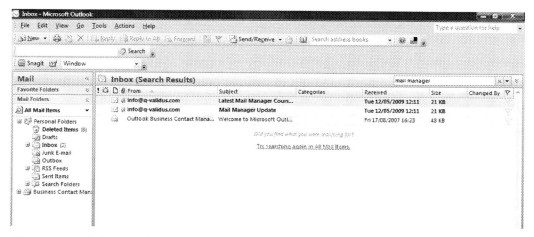

All instances of the search text entered are displayed and highlighted in the *Inbox (Search Results)*.

 It is good practice to always use meaningful subject titles in your emails, as it will really save time when you are searching for an email.

You can quickly reuse previous search phrases by selecting *Recent Searches* from the *Search* list menu and clicking the required search phrase.

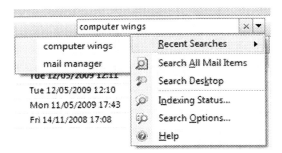

You can use the additional search criteria to refine your search results. This is useful if you are working with repetitive information, but only want to display information during a specific period.

To perform a search using the advanced search features:

1. Select *Tools* and click *Instant Search*.

2. Select *Advanced Find*.

3. In the *Advanced Find* dialogue box, input your search criteria in the available tabs.

4. You can search for any Outlook item, appointments and meetings, contacts, files, messages and notes, by using the *Look in* drop-down.

5. Select the folder you wish to search in by clicking *Browse*

6. Click on *Find Now*.

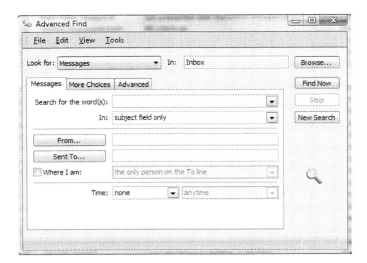

Quick Quiz

Select the correct answer from the following multiple-choice questions:

1   Within Outlook, selecting the key combination *Ctrl + Shift + N* will create a:

a   New Message

b   New Note

c   New Reminder

d   New Task

2   What does the following symbol represent?

a   A recurring task

b   A replied-to email

c   A deleted item

d   A completed task

3   Under which of the following menus can the *Out of Office Assistant* be accessed from?

a   *Edit*

b   *Tools*

c   *Actions*

d   *Go*

4   A rule in Outlook refers to?

a   A specific way to add appointments to the calendar

b   A particular way to mark entries in an address book

c   A series of tasks performed in a standard way on opening Outlook

d   A set of conditions that indicate specific actions are to be performed on a message meeting these conditions

Answers to Quick Quiz

1   b   New Note

2   a   A recurring task

3   b   *Tools*

4   d   A set of conditions that indicate specific actions are to be performed on a message meeting these conditions

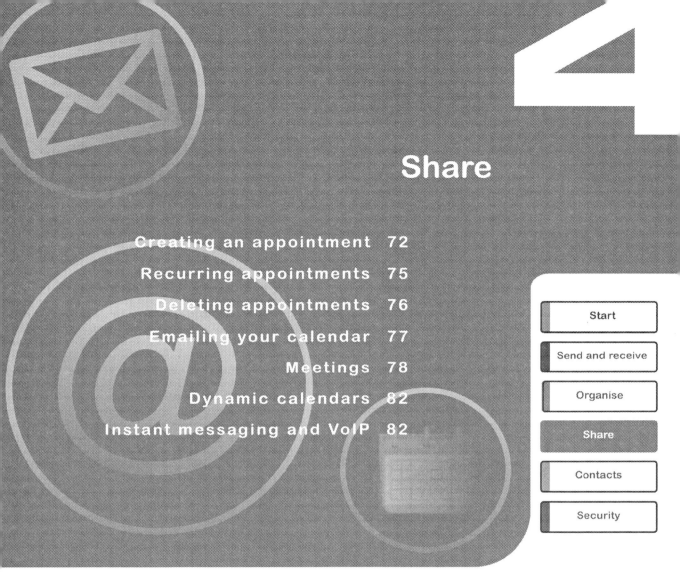

Share

Start

Send and receive

Organise

Share

Contacts

Security

Measuring points

- Create appointments in the calendar
- Add appointment reminders
- Add different notes for free / busy information
- Create, modify a recurring, one-off appointment.
- Delete appointments, events
- Email a calendar
- Interact to book, confirm, or re-schedule a meeting
- Print calendar in table, memo or calendar format
- Share, view calendars

- Send calendar information to a contact
- Create a meeting from scratch
- Create a meeting from an appointment
- Invite different people, request resources for the meeting
- Check meeting attendee response status
- Send a meeting update
- Be aware of different communication options such as instant messaging, VOIP (Voice over IP)

Introduction

Using the calendar feature in Outlook allows you to effectively manage your work schedule and appointments at a glance, particularly when multi-tasking on several different projects.

This chapter describes how you can schedule meetings and accept meeting requests, and share your calendar with other colleagues in a collaborative work environment. The chapter also covers some important concepts about Instant Messaging and the Voice over Internet Protocol (VoIP).

Create an appointment

You can use the Outlook calendar to schedule and manage your work activities and set up appointments. Any appointments that you schedule are displayed when you view your calendar.

To schedule an appointment in your calendar:

1. Select *File* and click *New*.

2. Click *Appointment*. or press *Ctrl+N*.

3. In the *Appointment* box add the required details:

    -   A name to identify the type of appointment.

    -   Location details.

    -   Start and end time details or select *All day event* to indicate that the event occurs all day.

    -   Any additional appointment details in the free text area.

4. Click *Save & Close*. The new appointment is displayed in your calendar.

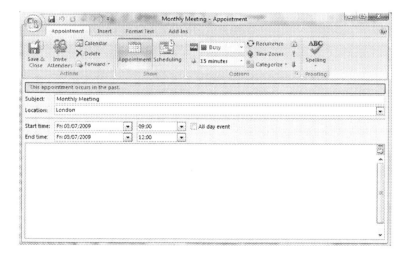

Setting a reminder

You can add a reminder to an existing appointment in your calendar and Outlook will automatically display this online reminder at any specified time prior to the actual appointment. There is a default reminder of 15 minutes automatically set before any meeting you arrange. You can set your own reminder as you wish prior to your appointments.

To set reminders:

1. Double-click on the appointment in your calendar.

2. Select the required *Reminder* for example, one hour prior to the appointment.

3. Click *Save & Close*.

A reminder notification is displayed in your calendar at the scheduled reminder time.

You can change the automatic default applied to appointments to suit your own work and schedule requirements, to do this:

1. Select *Tools* and click *Options*.

2. Select the required default setting. If you do not want reminders applied by default, deselect the *Default reminder* check box. You will have to manually specify any reminders in the individual appointment.

3. Click *Save & Close*.

Indicating availability

Prior to scheduling meetings in your calendar, you can view the availability of any person you plan to include in your meeting request, or show your own availability. When you work with your calendar and schedule different appointments, you can also indicate your busy and free times so that other colleagues can know about your availability.

 To support calendar availability your Outlook needs to be supported by the Microsoft Exchange Server version.

You can indicate to colleagues that you are not available by scheduling *Busy* time periods in your calendar.

To schedule a *Busy* time period:

1.   Select *File* and click *New*.

2.   Click *Appointment*.

3.   In the *Appointment* box, type or select the appointment details.

4.   In the appointment you can show your availability for others by choosing from:

     •   *Free*

     •   *Out of Office*

     •   *Busy*

     •   *Tentative*

 You can set a recurring appointment to indicate time periods when you are unavailable.

5.   Click *Save & Close*.

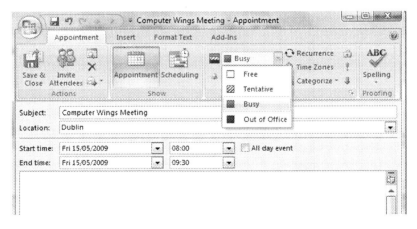

When your calendar is viewed by another colleague, for example, if they are creating a meeting request, your busy periods are displayed in the timelines that indicate meeting attendee availability.

Recurring appointments

The *Appointment Recurrence* feature allows you to set up appointments that will occur on a regular basis. It is worth while noting that to manage your time well you can also schedule a recurring busy period in your calendar, for example, if you want to block book a specific time period each day.

To create a recurring appointment:

1. Double-click on a date in your calendar to create an appointment.

2. Type a name for the appointment.

3. Click on the *Recurrence* icon.

4. In the *Appointment Recurrence* dialogue box, specify the time, recurrence pattern and range of recurrences for the appointment.

5. Click *OK*.

6. Click *Save & Close*.

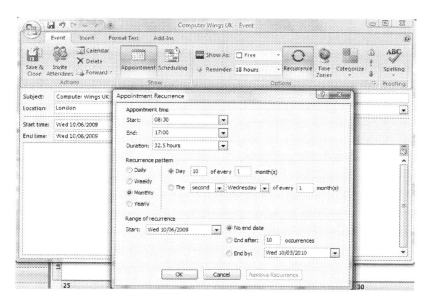

You can use the *Appointment Recurrence* feature to change a recurrent series and reflect that in your calendar. Details for a single appointment can be changed, without affecting the entire series, for example, every Monday morning can be the time for your management meetings except the 3rd Monday in March and July.

To modify a recurring appointment:

1. Select and open an appointment in your calendar by double-clicking it.

2. The *Open Recurring Item* dialogue box is displayed. Click *Open the series,* and then click the *Recurrence* icon.

3. In the *Appointment Recurrence* dialogue box, specify the required changes and click *OK.*

4. Specify the required time, recurrence pattern and range of recurrences for the appointment.

5. Click *OK.*

6. Click *Save & Close.*

Deleting appointments

To delete an appointment that is not a recurring appointment, click the *Delete* icon.

To delete a recurring appointment, use the following steps:

1. Select the required appointment in your calendar and click the *Delete* icon:

2. Select the appropriate option:

    –   *Open this occurrence* to delete the individual appointment.

    –   *Open the series* to delete the entire set of appointments.

3. Click *OK.*

Emailing your calendar

You can email your calendar information to your colleagues so that they are informed of your schedule. You can specify a date range and the level of information you want to include in your calendar.

To email your calendar:

1. Select *Calendar* in the *Navigation Pane* and click *Send a calendar via E-mail.*

2. Set the date range and the level of detail for the calendar extract you wish to send. For example, if you want the entire calendar to be sent, or a high level summary showing *Free, Busy, Tentative* and *Out of Office* times. You can also set your working hours so that only calendar information relating to this time period is emailed.

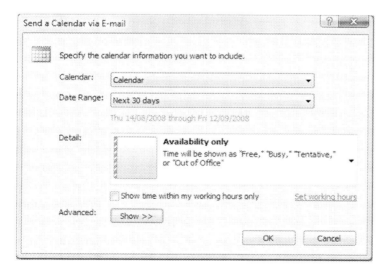

3. Click *OK*. Your calendar details are displayed in an email.

4. Review and check these details to ensure that you are only emailing information that you want to send to your colleagues.

5. Enter the recipient's details.

6. Click *Send*.

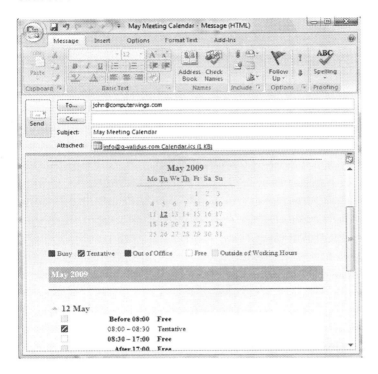

Meetings

An appointment is a time in your calendar when something is scheduled to happen. Within Outlook when you send invitations, choose and agree a location, add some resources, attach relevant documents, and manage participation, this is now considered as a meeting.

To schedule a meeting:

1. Select *File* and click *New,* or press *Ctrl+Shift+Q.*

2. Click *Meeting Request.*

3. Type the name of the meeting in the *Subject* text box and specify the meeting schedule details such as date, start and end times.

4. Specify where the meeting is being held in the *Location* field.

5. Specify any other information such as the meeting agenda in the free text area. You can also attach files that you want to share with the other attendees.

6. Select *Scheduling*.

7. Click *Add Others*.

8. Select *Add from Address Book*.

9. In *Select Attendees*, type the name of a person or resource that you want to invite to the meeting.

10. Check the scheduling of attendees to make sure there is no conflict with other appointments.

11. When you have completed all the details, click *Send* to email the meeting request.

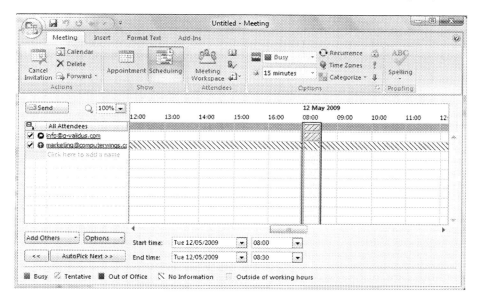

 In the illustration, the timelines are highlighted. If there is a conflict, you can check other times that are available and drag the timelines to the more favourable time. The times are reflected in the date, start and end times.

You can quickly convert an appointment to a meeting, to do this:

1. Open the appointment in your calendar.

2. Click on *Invite Attendees*. The appointment is converted into a meeting request.

3. Select the contacts you want to invite to the meeting.

4. Click *Send*.

Accept

To accept a meeting request:

1. Open the meeting request in your calendar.

2. Click *Accept*.

The meeting appointment is added to your calendar and is displayed as a busy time to prevent another appointment from being scheduled.

Check responses

You can check on the responses to a meeting to see if the time suits.

To check the meeting status:

1. Open the meeting request in your calendar.

2. Click the *Scheduling* tab, select your meeting to review the responses.

Rescheduling

You may find it necessary to reschedule a meeting and send a notification to all attendees.

To reschedule a meeting:

1. Double-click on meeting time on the calendar.

2. Modify the meeting details to reflect the change to the schedule.

3. Click *Send Update*.

Printing your calendar

You can print your Outlook calendar so that you have a hard copy available when your online calendar is not accessible, such as, when you are in a meeting or travelling or as a paper backup.

To print your calendar:

1. Open your calendar.

2. Select *File* and click *Print*.

3. Select the print style you want to apply to each page, for example, a print of one day per page.

   If you select the Tri-fold print style, it prints three adjacent views of your calendar as shown:

4. Specify the calendar date range you want printed.

5. Select *Preview* to check your calendar print style before printing it.

6. Click *OK*.

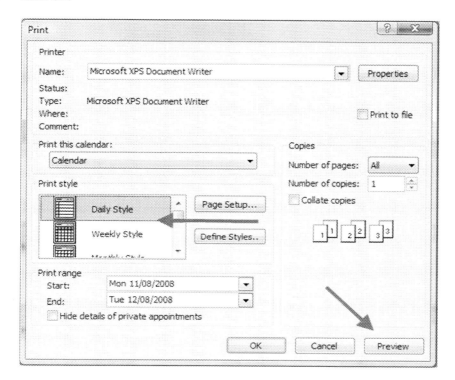

Dynamic calendars

You can share your Outlook calendar with your colleagues and view their shared calendars using Microsoft Exchange Server tools.

You can also choose to share the *Free/Busy* times from your calendar on Exchange Server so that meeting requests and information about your availability are dynamic.

To share a summary of your Free/Busy times, do the following:

1. Select *Tools* and click *Options*.

2. Select *Calendar Options*.

3. Select *Free/Busy Options*.

    By default, Outlook publishes two months of free/busy information and retrieves any updates every 45 minutes. You can change the existing details based on your preferences.

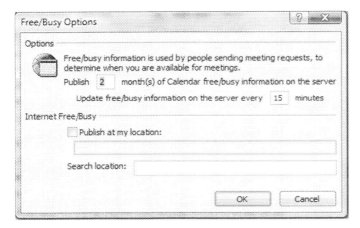

Instant messaging and VoIP

Communications methods are constantly evolving. Two communications options that have had a significant impact are Instant Messaging and VoIP.

● *Instant messaging* (IM): is a form of real-time text based communication between two or more people based on text. The text is conveyed over a network such as the Internet and is considered to be more of a real time chat/conversation unlike email.

● *Voice over Internet Protocol (VoIP)*: describes technologies that are used for delivering communications over the public telephone network, the Internet etc. Skype is an example of VoIP service that is widely used. Skype and different web conferencing tools allow users to communicate freely and to share resources over the internet at significantly lower cost.

Quick Quiz

Select the correct answer from the following multiple-choice questions:

1   What is the default reminder time setting for appointments in Outlook?

   a   1 hour

   b   15 mins

   c   2 hours

   d   2 days

2   What colour is associated with busy time in a Outlook calendar?

   a   Green

   b   White

   c   Blue

   d   Red

3   What happens if the keyboard shortcut *Ctrl+Shift+Q* is selected within Outlook?

   a   A meeting request form opens

   b   An appointment is booked into the calendar

   c   A note is inserted into the working document

   d   A question mark is inserted into the calendar

4   Which one of the following formats is a calendar print style?

   a   Hour style

   b   Day style

   c   Tri-fold style

   d   Yearly style

5   What does the acronym VoIP stand for?

   a   Value over International Protocol

   b   Voice over Internet Protocol

   c   Voice over Internal Protocol

   d   Value over Internal Protocol

Answers to Quick Quiz

1   b   15 mins

2   c   Blue

3   a   A meeting request form opens

4   c   Tri-fold

5   b   Voice over Internet Protocol

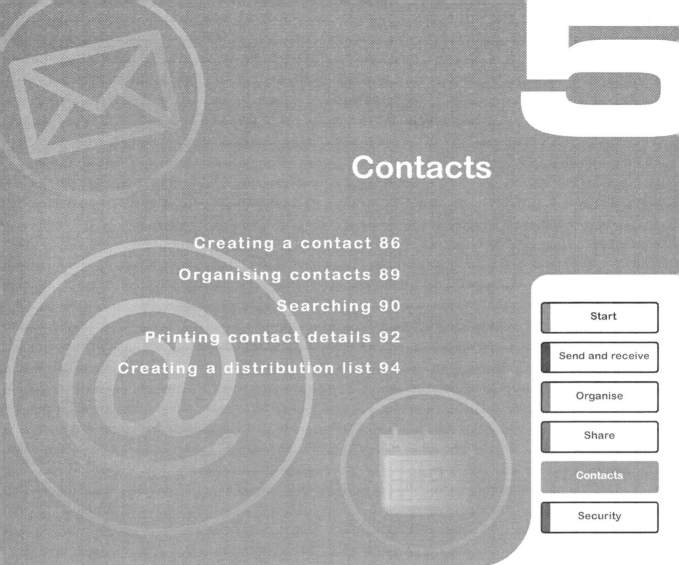

Contacts

Start

Send and receive

Organise

Share

Contacts

Security

Measuring points

- Create a contact
- Switch between different contact views: business, address card
- File, save a contact
- Add phone, mail, web and email information
- Enhance contact details with a picture
- Create a contact from an email message
- Find a contact categorise a contact: business, personal etc

- Share a contacts folder
- Print contacts using different print styles
- Create an address list
- Use contacts to create an address list, a distribution list and make changes
- Include a contacts folder in an address book
- Import data from an existing email client
- Import data from other applications

Introduction

Outlook enables you to quickly build and maintain a comprehensive list of contacts. Maintaining an up-to-date contacts list improves efficiency, and allows you to be more productive.

This chapter describes how you can add to and develop your contacts, and how you easily view and find your contacts. Outlook also allows you to share your contacts and work with address and distribution lists. Importing data from another email and other applications is also covered.

Create a contact

The *Contacts* folder acts as an address book where you can store the names and details of personal and business contacts.

To create a new contact:

1. Select *New* and click *Contact* or press *Ctrl+N*.

2. Specify the contact details in the contact form, such as phone, email address details and web details or additional information.

3. Click *Save & Close* to file the contact.

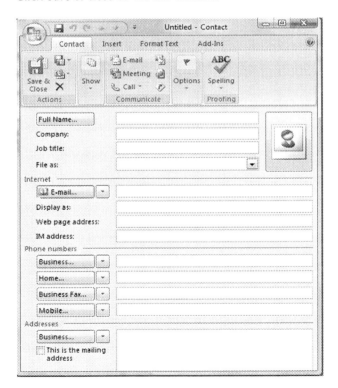

Switching views

You can display contact information in different views as you work in Outlook to suit your requirements.

To select a view:

1.   Select *Contacts*, click *Current View*.

2.   Select the required view from the list menu in the left hand pane.

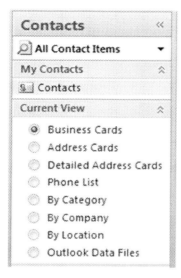

When you select *Business Cards*, the following view is displayed:

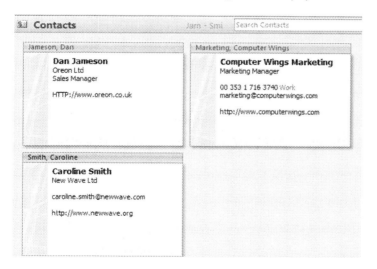

Adding a picture

You can add a picture to the details for a contact.

1. Open the contact form.

2. Click the *Picture* icon:

3. Navigate and select the required image file.

4. Click *OK*.

Save a contact

To save a contact, enter details in the contact form, and then click *Save & Close*.

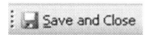

Building your contacts

You can use the details in an email to quickly develop your contacts.

To add a contact from an email:

1. Select and right-click on the email address.

2. Select *Add to Outlook Contacts*.

3. Add any other required details to the contact information.

4. Click *Save & Close*.

Organising contacts

In Outlook there are various options for how you can organise and display your contacts.

To set display and filing options for your contacts:

1. Select *Tools* and click *Options*.

2. Click *Contact Options*.

3. In the Contact Options dialogue box, set the required settings for displaying and filing your contact names.

4. Enable the *Check for Duplicates* check box to prevent duplicates occurring in your contact list.

5. Click *OK*.

Searching

As you build your contacts list, you can use the sort and *Search* features in Outlook to quickly find a specific contact. You can use the *Search* features in the contact list by:

- *Search address books* field.

- *Search Contacts* field.

Alternatively, you can view the contact information in columns and use the *Sort* feature.

You can also use the additional search options available in the *Tools* menu to perform more extensive searches in a contacts list.

Sharing

You can share your contacts by either:

- Forwarding a copy of one or more contacts in an email as an attachment. All the contact's details are sent.

- Creating and sharing contacts as Electronic Business Cards, a vCard.

vCards

You can use Versitcards (or vCards) for sharing contact information. A vCard is the standard file format for sharing business card information.

To send contact information as a vCard:

1. Open *Contacts*.

2. Select and right-click the required contact.

3. Select *Send Full Contact*.

4. Click *In Internet Format (vCard)*. A new email is displayed with the vCard attachment.

5. Type your message and click *Send*.

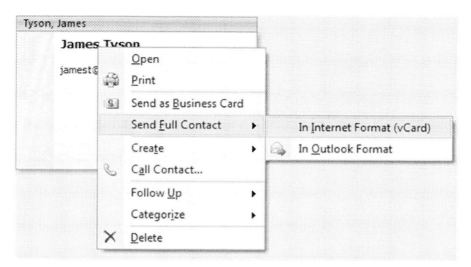

Exchange Server

If you are using an email account based on Exchange Server 2007, you can share your Contacts folder with colleagues.

1. In the *Navigation Pane*, select *Share My Contacts Folder* to launch an email message.

2. Specify any contacts that you want to share and click *Send*.

3. When prompted by Outlook, confirm that you want to share your contacts folder.

When the email is received, the recipient selects *Open this Contacts Folder* to view the contents of the contact folder. When you have shared your contact folder, you can modify its share permissions by right-clicking and select *Change Sharing Permissions*.

Printing contact details

You can print a copy of your contact details. This is useful if you want to store a copy for your records. You can choose from various print styles that set the appearance of the contact information.

You can view how the contact information is formatted based on the print style select using the *Preview* feature.

One option available is the *Card style* format, which displays contact information in card format. The contact list is compiled alphabetically:

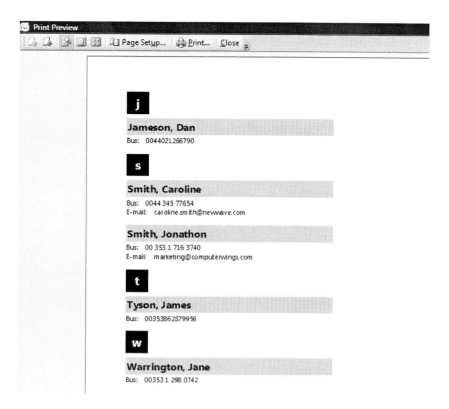

Another option is the *Small Booklet style* which is a customised version of the *Card style* and displays the individual contact details in a small booklet format:

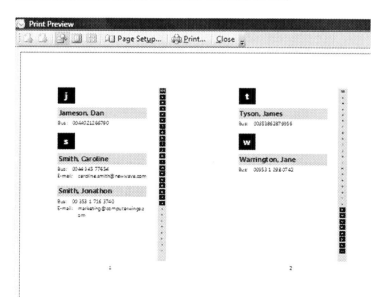

Create a distribution list

You can group one or more contacts into a distribution list. This is useful if you frequently distribute information to the same group, or if you want a distribution list for a particular team within your organisation.

To create a distribution list:

1. Select *File* and click *New* or press *Ctrl+Shift+L*.

2. Select *Distribution List*.

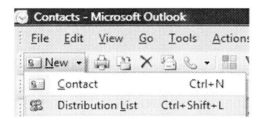

3. Type a name in the *Name* field.

4. Select *Distribution List* and click *Select Members*.

5. Select the required address book from the list.

6. Locate the contact name either by navigating to the name or using *Search*.

7. Select the name and then click *Members*.

8. Repeat steps 6-7 above for any other contacts you want to add.

9. Click *Save & Close* when you have selected all the members you want to include in the distribution list.

The distribution list is saved in your *Contacts* folder.

 In organisations that use an Exchange Server, common distribution lists can be created and accessed from an organisation's Global Address List (GAL).

Modify a distribution list

You can edit an existing distribution list to add or remove contacts. This is useful when members of a team change and you need to reflect the changes in the distribution list.

To update a distribution list:

1.   Open the required distribution list in your contact folder.

2.   Select *Distribution List* and click *Select Members* to select a contact name.

3.   Select the required contact and click on *Add New* or *Remove* as necessary.

4.   Click *Save & Close*.

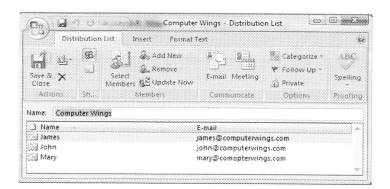

Importing contacts

Working in a collaborative environment with different project teams you many need to import contact information from other software applications and programs.

To import contact information from another application into your computer:

1. Select *File* and click *Import and Export*.

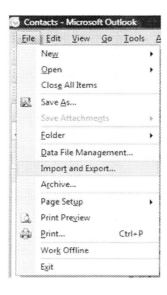

2. In the *Import and Export Wizard*, select *Import from another program or file* and click *Next*.

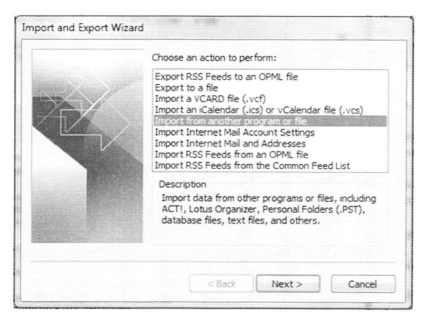

3. Review the list of applications and programs for which an import file can be created.

4. Click *Browse* and navigate to select the file you want to import.

5. Specify the folder in which you want to store the imported data.

6. Click *Finish*.

Quick Quiz

Select the correct answer from the following multiple-choice questions:

1 Which one of the following command sequences will file a contact?

    a   *General > Close*

    b   *Save > Close*

    c   *Save > File*

    d   *File > Folder*

2 What would you be intending to do if you clicked on this icon?

    a   Add details to a form

    b   Send a contact a message

    c   Add an image to a form

    d   Retrieve a contact

3 Insert the words to complete the following sentence?

A vCard is an _____ _____ _____ in a format that is understood by Outlook.

    a   Electronic Business Card

    b   Secure Contact Form

    c   Electronic Journal Entry

    d   Secure Address List

4 Which of the following is a print style that can be used to print Outlook Contacts?

    a   Preview Style

    b   Small Booklet Style

    c   Book Style

    d   Telephone Book Style

Answers to Quick Quiz

1 b   *Save > Close*

2 c   Add an image to a form

3 a   Electronic Business Card

4 b   Small Booklet Style

Security

Start

Send and receive

Organise

Share

Contacts

Security

Measuring points

- View folder, item sizes
- Backup items, folders
- Set backup, archive intervals
- Use available automatic archive
- Exclude some items from backup
- Restore archived data
- Recognise significant security considerations for the organisation with regard to email clients
- Recognise common email issues such as SPAM, junk mail, chain mail and viruses, and adjust security settings to help deal with these
- Set security settings on a personal folder
- Request, set up a certificate
- Send a message using a certificate
- Send, receive a signed message. Send an encrypted message

- Save a sender's public key
- Set different email security or privacy options
- Set attachment handling and macro security properties
- Set virus protection
- Be aware of data protection legislation or conventions in your country
- Be aware of copyright laws and their impact for downloading content from the Internet
- Be aware of 'netiquette' conversions and protocols for confidentiality when communicating with others
- Recognise guidelines and procedures set by the employer or the organisation
- Recognise the significance of disability / equality legislation in helping to provide all users with access to information

Introduction

Outlook has a range of features to ensure you manage your email effectively, from checking and limiting the size of folders, setting up routine back up folders and using automatic archiving for storing old emails and freeing up space.

This chapter covers the various types of email threats such as viruses and malicious software and the protection measures to counter them. Also the chapter deals with how you can apply email signatures and digital certificates to verify your online identity. Social conventions, organisational email policy and relevant legislation is also covered.

Managing folders and file sizes

As you work with Outlook, the amount of data storage used increases. You will need to carefully manage the storage space available to ensure that you avoid problems due to lack of space.

You should routinely check the size of an Outlook folder to ensure that you have sufficient space.

To check the size of your Inbox, for example:

1. Select and right-click the *Inbox* folder.

2. In the *Properties* box, click *General*.

3. Click *Folder Size*. The folder size is displayed with details of the total size including and excluding subfolders.

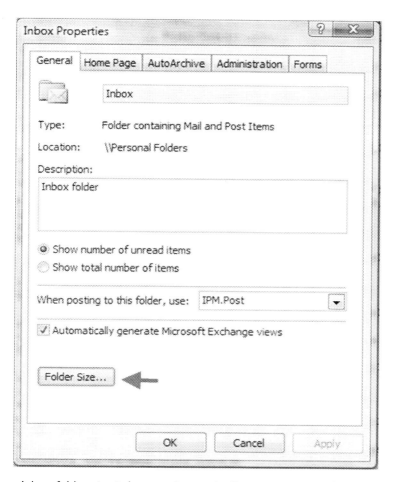

If your Inbox folder size is large and near the limit, go to your inbox, and sort emails by *Size* to identify the large emails and move and delete as required.

If this field is not displayed, select *View, Current View* and click *Customize Current View*. In the *Customize Current View* dialogue box, select *Fields*, select *Size* and click on *Add*. You can adjust where the *Size* column is displayed using the *Move Up* and *Move Down* buttons or by selecting the column and dragging it to the required location.

To check the size of your personal folders:

4.   To view the size of your personal folders, select *Personal Folders* from the *All Mail Items* list, in the left hand pane.

5.   Select *Properties for "Personal Folders"*, the details for individual folders are displayed.

       You can scroll through the list of folders to display folder details and click *Folder Size* to review size details.

6.   Click *OK* when finished.

You can perform these steps for other folders such as Contacts, Calendar and Tasks.

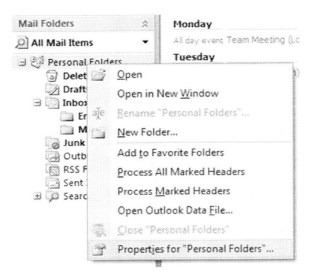

Backing up information

Backup is the routine procedure to store or archive important information for secure retrieval later.

It is good practice to monitor the size of your email folders, as you can easily reach your folder size quota, which is set by your network administrator, without realising it.

You can manage and organise information by:

- Creating backups of your personal folders to your hard disk or a network folder.

- Creating an export file containing information from your Outlook folders. Files must be exported individually.

- Using the *Archive* feature to move items from folders after a certain time period, every three or six months.

 The file extension for Outlook email folders is .pst.

Using backup

Outlook has a range of backup features to make sure you do not lose any of your emails files. Before you perform your backup, you should check the file size of any folder you are backing up to make sure there is available capacity on the backup storage media.

Microsoft offers a free Personal Folder Backup tool, which can be used to backup your entire .pst file.

You can download the tool from Microsoft Office Online website, just click download and follow the instructions. When you have downloaded and restarted Outlook, you will then see the *Backup* command included in the *File* menu.

To create a backup:

1. Select *File* and click *Backup*.

    The *Outlook Personal Folders Backup* box displays:

    *   The files that are included in the backup.

    *   When the last backup was performed.

2. Click *Options* to specify the files you want to include in the backup. You can add additional folders by navigating and selecting the folder and then clicking *Open*.

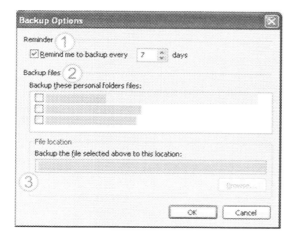

3. In the *Backup Options* dialogue box, set up an automatic reminder to remind you to make a backup by enabling the *Remind me to backup every x days* check box.

4. Specify the intervals when you want a reminder displayed where x is the number of days. Any number between 1 and 999 is permitted.

5. Choose required file in *Backup files* and select the *File location*.

6. Click *OK*.

7. Click *Save Backup*.

Backups of the selected items are created when you next exit Outlook.

Using AutoArchive

With AutoArchive, you can decide when you want information moved or deleted from your folders.

This feature allows you to free up space in folders that you are actively using, while maintaining information in a location where it can be easily accessed.

To specify AutoArchive options:

1. Select *Tools* and click *Options*.

2. Click *Other*.

3. Click *AutoArchive*.

4. Complete the required details:

   a. The number of days between each archive.

   b. If you want to automatically delete items older than, for example, 3 months, select 3 in the *Clean out items older than* option.

   c. The target file where archived items are to be transferred *Move old items to*. You can specify an existing file or use *Browse* to locate and select a specific file.

5. Click *OK*.

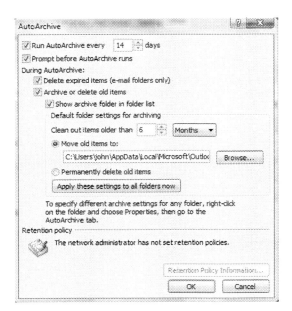

You can change your AutoArchive interval at any point.

If you wish to exclude certain items from your regular archive routine, use the following steps:

1. Open the required item, click the *Office* icon and select *Properties*.

2. Select *Do not AutoArchive this item*.

3. Click *OK*.

4. Close the item.

5. Click *Save*.

The final step is to validate your archive, which can only be done by restoring from the archive.

Restoring archived data

The value of an archive is based on the actual retrieval of the information.

To retrieve archived information:

1. Select *File* and click *Open*.

2. Select *Outlook Data File*.

3. In *Open Outlook Data File*, locate and select the file you want to restore.

4. Click *OK*. The selected file is displayed in your folder list. You can expand the file, by clicking on + to navigate to a specific file.

5. Select and drag the email content back to the required location.

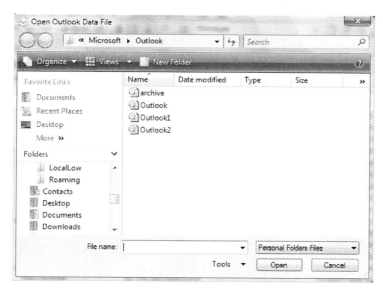

Security

Email is a significant feature of modern communication, and individuals and organisations are all increasingly reliant on email. Increases in usage have been accompanied by a corresponding growth in email security threats.

While Windows Operating Systems and applications such as Outlook incorporate some specific security features, everyone using email needs to be aware of the existing and new threats. The main email security threats are viruses, spam, phishing and spyware.

Viruses

A computer virus is a malicious program that copies itself between computers and infects them. The programs can cause significant damage to your local computer or to your organisation's network.

Viruses have become very sophisticated in recent years. Early viruses would execute the file and run, when the email attachment was opened. Today a virus can be embedded in an email so that it will launch automatically when just the email is opened.

SPAM

Unsolicited email is known as SPAM, or junk mail. SPAM is email sent indiscriminately and often for commercial purposes. SPAM is also used to hide malicious viruses that can harm your computer environment. Another form of SPAM is chain mail, where the recipients are encouraged to pass on an email to numerous contacts, with some emotional manipulation involved.

Phishing

Phishing is an attempt to obtain details about an individual's identity for the purpose of performing fraud. Recipients are encouraged to enter their personal information on what may be a fictitious version of a commercial website, such as a bank, that have been illegally created for the purposes of fraud.

Spyware

Spyware is a computer program that is installed on a computer without the knowledge of its owner. It is used to collect information about the user's behaviour, for example, their Internet and other applications usage. It can change settings on a user's computer so that software applications no longer work as expected.

Working with attachments

When you work with attachments, you need to take certain precautions to avoid introducing any possible threats. You should treat all email attachments with caution:

- It is good practice to use the AutoPreview feature for incoming attachments in Outlook.

- Any attachment received, even from trusted colleagues should be virus checked.

- Unsolicited attachments received from colleagues should be virus scanned or checked with the sender to determine the integrity of the attachment.

- Delete any files which are not work related, such as jokes.

- Delete any emails and attachments from unknown or unsolicited sources.

Many of these standard practices when working with email should be part of the organisational email policies.

Security on personal folders

You can set a password on a personal folder to restrict access to the information contained in the folder.

To set a password:

1. Select your personal folder.

2. Click *Properties* and select *Advanced*.

3. In the *Personal Folders* dialogue box, click on *Change Password*.

4. Type and confirm your password.

5. Click *OK*.

 If your personal folder is stored on a network drive, you should contact your network administrator before setting or changing password restrictions.

Digital certificates

Sending and receiving emails securely involves providing verification of your identity and a guarantee that information in the email has not been altered during transmission. Digital certificates provide a digital signature which are used in emails to verify and guarantee the identification of the email sender, and they are the online equivalent of traditional handwritten signatures.

 Before you begin the process of obtaining a digital certificate, you should contact your network administrator.

Obtaining a digital certificate

You can obtain a digital certificate from a certificate authority (CA). VeriSign and Thawte are examples of companies that supply digital signatures and a range of other authentication and encryption certificates.

You can obtain your own digital certificate from your preferred CA supplier by signing on to their websites and completing the secure purchasing process. When you have obtained a certificate, you need to set up the certificate in Outlook.

The purchasing process will vary with different vendors, the initial steps are carried out in the *Trust Center*:

1.   Select *Tools* and click *Trust Center*.

2.   Select *E-mail Security* on the left hand pane, click *Set a Digital ID*.

     Outlook opens your web browser to a page on the Microsoft Office Online website.

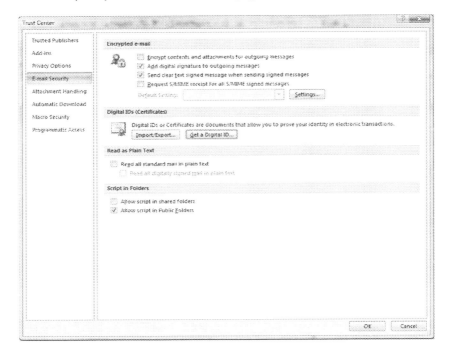

3.   Choose the third-party provider you want and click on their website link.

4.   Complete the purchasing requirements on the providers website and then follow the instructions in the email sent to you on completion of the purchase, to install the digital ID on your computer..

When your certificate is installed, you can make it available in Outlook.

To activate a digital certificate you need to find and validate it:

1.   Select *Tools* and click *Trust Center*.

2.   Select *Email Security*.

3.	Click *Settings*.

4.	In the *Change Security Settings* dialogue box, type a name for your settings.

5.	Click *OK* to save this setting.

6.	Click *Choose* to select the certificate from the list that you want to use.

	You can display each certificate using *View Certificate*.

7.	Select the certificate you want to use and click *OK*.

8.	In the *Change Security Settings* dialogue box, validate the certificate is available and choose your requirements, whether certificate is to be used for signing, encryption or both, click *OK*.

Now every time you open a new email message you will see some security icons associated with the digital certificate.

Using your digital certificate

When you have obtained and defined your digital certificate, you can use them to verify your identity as well as encrypting your emails.

Emails that have been digitally signed can still be intercepted and read. If you want to ensure that only the recipient can read the message, you need to use encryption.

To use encryption, you need a copy of the digital certificate for the intended recipient. You can obtain this signature by storing a copy of the individual's digital signature from an email to their contact details in your contact list.

To send an email with a digital certificate:

1.	Create a new email and the following icons are displayed:

	Signing Icon

	Selecting this icon will allow you to sign your email with your chosen digital certificate.

	Encrypting Icon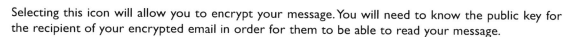

	Selecting this icon will allow you to encrypt your message. You will need to know the public key for the recipient of your encrypted email in order for them to be able to read your message.

2.	Click on the icons as required depending on your security requirements.

3.	Your signature is applied to the email and verifies your identity to your recipient.

Saving a sender's public key

In order to encrypt a message, you need to record the public key which is part of the digital certificate information for your intended recipient.

To save the public key for a contact:

1. Open an email with the digital signature.

2. Select *From* and click on *Add to Contacts*.

3. For an existing contact, select *Update new information from this contact to the existing one*. The certificate details are added to the contact information.

You can open a digital signature from a contact by opening the contact details and clicking on *Certificates*.

Macro security

Macros are a program written in Microsoft Visual Basic and activated when a document is opened. Macros are used to automate certain tasks that are performed regularly.

Macros can be used maliciously and trigger what is known as a macro virus when the file attachment is opened.

Macros are often found as part of Word template documents. When you open a document containing a macro, a warning will alert you to the existence of macros and to check if you want to continue.

Outlook cannot alert you to the presence of macro viruses as they are included in attachments and not directly in emails. To protect your computer, you should set your security level to *High* to ensure that only macros from trusted sources are permitted to run.

To check the default Outlook security setting:

1. Select *Tools* and click *Trust Center*.

2. Click *Marco Security*.

3. Select your required setting, and click *OK*.

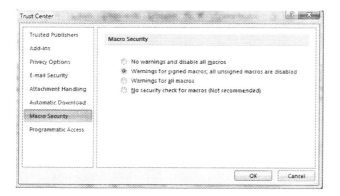

Address book security

An alert is automatically displayed if a program attempts to access your Outlook Address book. This is to prevent transmission of emails from an unauthorised source. The alert notifies you about the access attempt and prompts you to confirm whether access should be permitted or blocked.

Where the access attempt is from a legitimate source, you can specify a duration for the access and select *Yes*, for example, if you have started a program that needs to access your Address book, select *No* where you are unaware of any legitimate access from a recognised source.

 This alert is not displayed by Outlook where the access is a trusted update.

You should use additional security features to safeguard against possible threats, such as antivirus software. In most large organisations, this protection is usually enforced at network level. Contact your network administrator for further details of security arrangements in your organisation.

Netiquette

'Netiquette' stands for Internet Etiquette and refers to the set of rules and practices that should be followed and applied when communicating online. Communicating clearly on the Internet without creating confusion and misunderstandings can sometimes be challenging.

The unofficial rules and practices of netiquette have evolved over time and are designed to ensure that email communication is courteous and inoffensive. The following are some of the standard guidelines:

- Make sure that your recipient addresses are correct otherwise messages may be sent to the wrong people or may bounce back to you.

- Use organisational distribution lists where appropriate.

- Only send emails to relevant people. Avoid the tendency to copy others in on emails unnecessarily.

- Always include a subject line in your email. The subject should be concise and appropriate. This will enable the recipient to understand the content of your email and will also help avoid your email being treated as SPAM.

- Think carefully about applying Carbon copy (Cc) addresses as email recipients may not wish their email addresses to be known to others. If addresses are sensitive use the hidden addresses (Blind carbon copy of Bcc) function. Do not over use Bcc.

- Be careful about what you write and what information you put in an email. Avoid sending confidential information by email. Once you have written your email message and sent it, you will have no control over where your email may go. Consider all your email messages to be public and act accordingly.

- Make sure to use appropriate greetings when addressing your recipient.

- Keep your message brief. Try not to exceed one screen view. If your message is short people are more likely to read it. Remember many people now receive emails on mobile devices.

- Be careful with emotions, such as, humour or anger. Remember what one person finds humorous another may find offensive. Your email will not go away when you hit the delete key and may be used against you later. Do not write in CAPS as it looks as if you are shouting.

- Use appropriate grammar and use the spell check function before sending your email.

- If sending an attachment, attach the file first. Too often emails are composed and the sender forgets to attach the file and has to resend the email later. Be careful of sending large files or multiple files with an email.

- Do not send attached files internally if those files can be found in a shared location in the organisation's network. Advise your work colleagues where the files can be found in the network.

- Always include your email address and contact details on your emails. Apply organisational house styles as required.

- When replying to an email consider if you need to reply in the first instance and, if so, who you need to reply to. Avoid unnecessary use of the *Reply to All* command.

- Read and respond to emails at set times during the working day so that email does not continuously intrude on your work.

- Apply the Out of Office feature if you are away from the office for a prolonged period of time.

Data protection legislation

National data protection legislation defines the legal basis for the handling of personal information in a particular country and provides the basis by which individuals can govern the control of information about themselves. Such legislation typically confers rights on individuals who have their personal information stored as well as obligations on those who store such data.

The principles of data protection require that personal data should be processed fairly and lawfully. In order for data to be classed as fairly processed, at least one of the following six conditions must be applicable to the data:

- The data subject (the person whose data is stored) has consented to the processing.

- Processing is necessary for the performance of a contract (any processing not directly required to complete a contract would not be fair).

- Processing is required under a legal obligation (other than one stated in the contract).

- Processing is necessary to protect the vital interests of the data subject's rights.

- Processing is necessary to carry out any public functions.

- Processing is necessary in order to pursue the legitimate interests of the data controller or third parties (unless it could unjustifiably prejudice the interests of the data subject).

You should be aware of the applicable legislation in your own country.

Copyright and the Internet

Copyright material published on the Internet will generally be protected in the same way as material in other media. Copyright is protected internationally through international treaties, such as, the Berne Convention to which over 160 countries are parties to. Before the Berne Convention, national copyright laws usually only applied for works created within each country.

Copyright has two main purposes, namely the protection of the author's right to obtain commercial benefit from valuable work and the protection of the author's general right to control how a work is used. Almost all works are copyrighted the moment they are written and no copyright notice is required.

You should be aware that if publishing material from other sources the express permission of the copyright owner (unless copyright exceptions apply) is required. In all cases, copies should be acknowledged as far as is practicable. In addition, many websites will include a copyright statement setting out exactly the way in which materials on the site may be used.

You should also be aware that many online resources may have been published illegally without the permission of the copyright owners. Any subsequent use of the materials, such as printing, or copying and pasting, may also be illegal.

For further details on copyright requirements within your own country please refer to your own applicable national legislation.

Disability / equality legislation

Disability legislation prohibits direct discrimination, victimisation and harassment and promotes equality for disabled people. Disability legislation, in particular, makes it unlawful to discriminate against people in respect of their disabilities in relation to such matters as employment, the provision of goods and services, education and transport.

At national level, policies relating to people with disabilities reflect the diversity of cultures and legislative frameworks in the EU Member States. The definitions and the criteria for determining disability are currently laid down in national legislation and administrative practices and differ across the current Member States according to their perceptions of, and approaches to, disability.

You should be aware of your own applicable national legislation as well as relevant international directives.

Quick Quiz

Select the correct answer from the following multiple-choice questions:

1   Which one of the following is procedures backup email messages in Outlook?

   a   Double-click the message and save

   b   Use the export facility

   c   Click *Go* then select *Tasks*

   d   Click *Actions* then select *Categorise*

2   Which one of the following characterises the term 'phishing'?

   a   Identity theft using email

   b   Removing cookies from a computer

   c   Infecting a computer with a virus

   d   Attaching files to an email

3   A _____ _____ is a form of verification that guarantees that a mail wasn't changed between the sender's machine and the recipient's machine.

   Choose the missing words to complete the sentence from the options below:

   a   Personal certificate

   b   Identity certificate

   c   Digital certificate

   d   Machine certificate

4   A series of commands and instructions that are grouped together as a single command to accomplish a task automatically are also known as a:

   a   Task

   b   Menu

   c   Structure

   d   Macro

5   Which one of the following is an example of good practice in email communication?

a   Type messages in CAPITAL LETTERS only

b   Ensure the subject line reflects the content of the message

c   Where possible, attach large files when forwarding an email

d   Ensure you forward email advertising at every opportunity.

Answers to Quick Quiz

1   b   Use the export facility

2   a   Identity theft using email.

3   c   Digital certificate

4   d   Macro

5   b   Ensure the subject line reflects content of the message